The Ladies Aid
of Santa Ynez

A
COOK
BOOK
1926

*Plus: Brief Biographical History of
Those Who Contributed Recipes.*

JIM NORRIS

The Ladies Aid of Santa Ynez

A
Cook
Book
1926

Plus: Brief Biographical History of Those Who Contributed Recipes.

JIM NORRIS

OLIVE PRESS - P.O. BOX 99 - LOS OLIVOS CA. 93441

iv

ISBN 0-933380-26-7

First printing 1983.

The Olive Press Publications
P. O. Box 99
Los Olivos, California 93441

Production: D & J Litho, Los Angeles

DEDICATION

Two young-thinking women were particularly helpful
in the development of this book.

MYRTLE EDSELL BUELL

Myrtle offers a broad knowledge of the Santa Ynez
Valley plus her personal association with many
Valley history-makers.

Most infectious - her wonderful laugh - completely
disarming.

OLIVIA GUIDOTTI JENSEN

Olivia also provides an extremely rich background.
Growing up in four Valley communities, she has
known many people. Her quiet manner and gentle
smile do not foretell her wealth of stories.

Pleasant days to both

INTRODUCTION

Why get involved with a cook book?

The 79 contributors (78 females and 1 male) represent a wide diversity of cultures and ethnic backgrounds plus pioneering spirit.   If you examine the history of the women, you are immediately impressed by their long lives. Was this longevity due to the Valley climate? The water? The personal hardships? The help they offered one another? (The Ladies Aid, for instance.) Good food? Love of life? Closeness with nature? Hardy stock?

You will draw your own conclusions.

1926 was an "up" year in the Santa Ynez Valley; midway between World War I and the Depression. Old ranches were expanding and new ranches being developed. Those growing up locally knew everyone and often intermarried. (Newcomers are sometimes admonished: "Don't talk about anyone - they are all related.")

It is these inter-relationships that are so fascinating.

The Ladies Aid participated in sewing and quilting to raise funds for the Presbyterian Church; non-denominational in 1926. As far as anyone can remember, this was the first cook book printed in the Valley. The Santa Ynez Valley News, then published by Oscar L. Powell, probably printed it. Again, the purpose was to raise funds.

About the recipes...

There were over twenty dairies in the Valley in 1926 - butter was cheap and PLENTIFUL! Those of you who are diet conscious --- take heed.

Some of the recipes show Myrtle Buell's corrections; others may need

CONTENTS

Santa Ynez Valley Ladies' Aid

Cook Book

Recipes contained in this Cook Book have been contributed by the women of Santa Ynez valley, and were compiled by the Ladies Aid Society of the Santa Ynez Presbyterian church, 1926.

The Ladies Aid Cook Book Committee:

MRS. F. M. KILMER, JR.

MRS. S. K. McMURRAY

MRS. WILLIAM STEP

MRS. JAMES A. WESTCOTT

MRS. W. A. BARRETT, Chairman.

We may live without poetry, music and art;
We may live without conscience and live without heart;
We may live without friends; we may live without books;
But civilized man can not live without cooks.

He may live without books—what is knowledge but grieving?
He may live without hope—what is hope but deceiving?
He may live without love—what is passion but pining?
But where is the man that can live without dining?

—Owen Meredith

The Ladies Aid Society wish to express their sincere thanks to the women of Santa Ynez valley for their generous support in making this cook book possible through contributions of favorite recipes and orders for the book.

BEVERAGES

"We'll take a cup of kindness yet for Auld Lang Syne."—R. Burns.

COFFEE FOR TWENTY

Take 24 tbsp coffee. Break the white of an egg over and stir thoroughly, put into cheesecloth bag in large coffee pot, pour over 10 cups cold water and let come to boil for 10 minutes. Add 10 cups boiling water and let boil 10 minutes longer. Set on back of stove where it will keep very hot, but not boil, for 20 minutes.

COCOA

Take 2 tbsp cocoa and 1 tsp sugar and 1 tbsp. water for each cup of milk. Mix cocoa, sugar and water and set over fire to boil for a few minutes. Add milk and serve when piping hot. Do not let the milk boil.

TEA

Allow 1 tsp. of tea to each cup of boiling water. Scald teapot, put in tea, pour on the boiling water and let stand from 3 to 5 minutes.

LEMONADE

One pound sugar to juice of 4 lemons and grated rind, allow 1 tbsp. to glass of water.

GRAPE PUNCH

To 1 pint grape juice add juice of 3 lemons and 1 orange and 1 cup sugar. Serve in glasses 1-3 full of chopped ice.

GRAPE JUICE PUNCH

Boil 1-2 cup water and 1 cup sugar together 7 minutes, add 1 quart water, 1 pint grape juice, juice of 2 lemons, 3 oranges, serve with ice.

COCOA SYRUP

Two cups water, 1 cup cocoa, 2 cups sugar, pinch of salt. Boil slowly 10 minutes, when cold bottle and set on ice. Take 2 tbsp. syrup for each glass of cold milk, top with whipped cream.

FRUIT PUNCH

Eight cups sugar boiled with water to make syrup. Cool and add the juice of 30 lemons, 18 oranges, 2 large cans of pineapple, 1-2 pound candied cherries. Then add 5 qts. water, put in a stone jar and add a large piece of ice. This should be about 12 quarts as the syrup and fruit should make 7 quarts. May add more water, as it is rather rich.

---X---

BREAD AND ROLLS

"Give us this day our daily bread"

POP OVERS

One cup flour, 1-2 tsp. salt, 1 cup milk, 2 eggs, 1 tsp. melted butter,, sift salt and flour together, add milk gradually, then eggs slightly beaten, and then melted butter. Beat with a Dover egg beater 5 minutes, pour quickly into hot buttered gem pans. Bake in hot oven 30 minutes.
Mrs. Katherine M. Hill

WALNUT BROWN BREAD

Two cups white flour, 1 1-2 cups graham flour, 1 tsp. salt, 1-2 cup of brown sugar, 1-2 cup molasses, 2 tbsp. melted butter, 1 egg, 2 cups sweet milk, 1 cup chopped nuts, 1 1-2 level tsp. baking soda.
Bake 1 hour in a moderate oven.
Mrs. Katherine M. Hill

BROWN BREAD

One pint sour milk, 1 scant tsp. soda, 1 cup white flour with 1 1-2 tsp. baking powder, 2 cups graham flour. Stir all together and pour into bread pan and bake 45 minutes or when tested no dough is seen. Add nuts, raisins, prunes, dates or figs, or any other fruit if liked.
Mrs. Nellie C. McMurray

CORN BREAD

Two cups yellow cornmeal, 1 cup wheat flour, 1 egg, 1 heaping tsp. baking powder, 1 level tsp soda. Sift cornmeal, flour, baking powder and soda, then stir in enough butter milk to make medium batter, add beaten egg. Put 2 tbsp. shortening in bake pan and melt, then pour in

the mixture. Beat thoroughly and bake in a rather hot oven.

Ione Jamison.

WAFFLES

Three eggs, 1 pint milk, 1-2 cup of melted butter, 2 cup flour, 2 tsp. of baking powder. Beat yolks until very light, add milk, then flour, then butter and baking powder. Beat hard and add egg whites and beat thoroughly. For 4 persons.

Mrs. F. M. Kilmer, Jr.

LEMON GEMS

One half cup sugar, 1-2 cup butter, 2 eggs, pinch of salt, 1 cup flour, 1 tsp. baking powder, grated rind and juice of 1 lemon. Cream sugar and butter, add egg yolks well beaten, and grated lemon rind. Sift together the salt, flour and baking powder and add beat well, then fold in the egg whites whipped stiff, then the lemon juice. Makes 8 gems. Bake in moderate oven.

David Westcott

CHEESE DROP BISCUITS

One half cup grated cheese, 1-4 tsp. salt, 1-2 cup water, 2 tbsp. melted butter, 1 cup flour, 3 level tsp. baking powder. Use a fork to mix ingredients. Drop by the spoonsful onto buttered tine. Bake 15 minutes in a hot oven.

Jessie S. Winter

SOUR MILK PANCAKES

Enough clabbered milk to make almost as much batter as you want, soda to sweeten, salt, 3 eggs and flour to make batter as thick as desired. Have griddle very hot and little greased.

Mrs. Ernest Mankins

BEATEN BISCUIT

One quart flour, 1-4 cup lard, 1-2 tsp. salt, 1 cup cold water. Rub the lard and salt into flour, and mix with water to a very stiff dough. Knead 10 minutes, or until well mixed. Then beat hard with a biscuit beater or rolling pin, turning the mass over and over until it begins to blister and look light and puffy. When in this condition, pull off a small piece suddenly, form in round biscuit, then pinch off a bit from the top. Turn over and press with thumb leaving a hollow in the center. Put biscuits some distance apart in the pan. Prick with fork. Bake 20 minutes in a quick oven. They should be light, of an even grain, and crack at edges like crackers.

Mrs. F. M. Kilmer, Jr.

..VIRGINIA SPOON CORN BREAD..

One cup corn meal 1 heaping tsp. baking powder, 1 level tsp. salt, 3 eggs beaten 1 minute, 2 cups sweet milk, 2 tbsp. melted bacon grease or butter. This makes almost a custard and is much nicer with nut meats. Serve with butter and honey.

Mrs. James A. Westcott

BAKED BROWN BREAD

One half cup flour, 2 eggs, 2 cups sour milk, 2 tsp. soda, 1 tsp, salt, 1-2 cup molasses, 2 1-2 cup graham flour, 1 cup whole wheat flour, 1 cup raisins; mix well and bake in covered tin 1 hour.

Susan Raymond

VIRGINIA CORN BREAD

Dissolve 1 tbsp. of butter in 3 1-2 pints of boiling milk, stir in 1 quart corn meal, when cool add 1 cup of wheat flour, 1 tsp. sugar, 1 tsp. salt and 2 well beaten eggs. Mix well and bake in 2 tins well buttered.

Mrs C. R. Weston

WAFFLES

One and three quarters cups of flour, 3 tsp. baking powder, pinch of salt, 3 tsp. sugar, 1 cup sweet milk, 2 eggs, 3 tbsp. melted butter. Sift together flour, salt and baking powder. Beat egg yolks until thick, add sugar and melted butter and then alternately add the milk to this and the flour, beat well, lastly fold in the 2 egg whites beaten stiff but do not beat. Bake in hot iron.

Mrs. T. F. Spalding

SWEET RUSKS

Two tbsp sugar, 1 cup milk, 2 tbsp. butter, 1-2 yeast cake, 1-4 tsp. salt, 4 cups flour, 1-2 cup lukewarm water. Cream butter and sugar, add well beaten yolks of - eggs and the stiffly beaten whites. Sift in flour and salt and add milk gradually. Add yeast dissolved in luke warm water, cover and let rise. When very light pour into buttered biscuit pan fill-

ing it half full. Let rise until pan is full. Bake in a moderate oven 20 minutes. When done, cut in long narrow strips.

Mrs. F. M KilmerJr.

CORN BREAD

Three fourths cup corn meal, 1 cup flour, 1-3 cup sugar, 1-2 tsp. of salt, 2 eggs well beaten, 1 cup sour milk, 1-2 tsp. soda, 2 tsp. baking powder, 3 tbsp. melted butter; mix in order given and bake in shallow buttered pans in quick oven.

Mrs. W. A. Barrett

NUT BREAD

Two cups graham flour, 2 cups white flour, 1 cup sugar, 1 tsp. salt, 4 tsp. baking powder, 1 cup chopped nuts, 2 cups milk, 2 cups milk, 1 egg well beaten. Put in greased pan, let stand in warm place 20 minutes. Bake 1 hour in slow oven, makes 2 loaves.

Mrs. W. H. Ellis

STEAMED BROWN BREAD

One cup sweet milk, 1 cup sour milk, 2 cups Indian meal, 1 cup raisins, 1 tsp. salt, 1 tsp. soda. Add milk to molasses, stir in soda and salt, add corn meal and flour, raisins last. Stir well. Grease 1 pound baking powder cans, fill 1-3 full, tightly cover and steam 1 1-2 hours.

Mrs. Myra W. Lyons

BOSTON BROWN BREAD

Two well beaten eggs, 3-4 cups of molasses, 1 tsp. salt, 2 cups buttermilk, 3 scant tbsp soda, 1 tsp. baking powder, 1-2 cup white flour, 1 1-2 cup corn meal, 1 cup graham flour, add 1 cup raisins if desired. Mix and steam 3 hours in buttered molds, fill molds only 2-3 full and keep cover on molds tightly, keep boiling water about to top of cans and fill up as needed, boiling constantly.

Mrs W. A. Barrett

CORN BREAD

Grate 3 dozen ears of corn, mix 1 cup sugar, 1 tsp. salt, 1 cup melted shortening, 1 cup milk. Mix all together and bake 1 hour, to be eaten hot.

Mrs Virginia Ontiveros

BOSTON BROWN BREAD

Mix 1 cup rye meal, 1 cup corn meal, 1 cup graham flour, 2 tsp. of soda and 1 tsp. salt. Add 3-4 cup molasses and 2 cups sour milk, beat well, put into well buttered molds and steam about 5 hours. Bake about 1-2 hour after removing from the steamer. The molds should never be more than 2-3 full. The cover should always be buttered.

Mrs. Jos. B. Miller

CINNAMON TOAST

Make as many slices of nice brown toast as you want. For each slice of toast, mix 1 tbsp. of sugar and 1-2 tsp. cinnamon. Butter the toast and sprinke cinnamon and sugar on it. Put slices of toast in shallow pan in moderate oven just a few minutes to melt the sugar and they are ready to serve.

B. E. K.

PARKER HOUSE ROLLS

Three tbsp. butter, 1 tsp. salt, 1-2 cup lukewarm water, 6 cups sifted flour, 1 pint milk, 1 tbsp. sugar, 1 cake yeast. Scald the milk and pour it over the sugar, salt and the butter. Allow it to cool, and when it is lukewarm, add the yeast, dissolved in lukewarm water, and then add 3 cups flour. Beat hard, cover and let rise until it is a frothy mass. Then add 3 more cups flour. Let rise again until it is twice its original bulk, then place it on your kneading board. Knead lightly and roll out 1-2 inch thick. Take a biscuit cutter and cut out the rolls. Brush each piece with butter fold and press edges together and place in greased pan 1 inch apart. Let them rise until very light. Bake in hot oven for 15 minutes.

Mrs. F. M. Kilmer Jr.

NUT BREAD

One cup flour, 1 tsp. baking powder, 1-4 cup sugar, 1 egg, 1-2 cup chopped walnuts, 1-2 tsp. salt. Mix into stiff dough with milk, put into buttered pans and let stand for 30 minutes. Bake in rather slow oven. Makes delicious sandwiches.

B. E. K.

SCOTCH SHORT BREAD

One pound flour, (take out 2 tbsp. and put in 2 tbsp. corn starch) 1-2 lb. butter, 1-3 lb. powdered sugar. Knead sugar into butter, then knead in the flour. Roll out bread until 1

For everyday needs of staples and special demands for fancy groceries see—

WATTS & LAUBLY

Cash Grocery

"Service With A Smile"

2 Telephones 91   Lompoc, Calif   P. O. Box 187

By specializing in groceries we offer a complete line. Remarkable assortment of imported and domestic Delicasies. 21 varieties of domestic and imported cheese. We cater to quantity purchases and are well equipped to ship out of town orders by mail or express.

inch thick. Prick all over with fork. Pinch edges with fingers and thumb across in 4 pieces. Bake in slow oven 45 minutes.

Mrs. F. M. Kilmer Jr.

SOUR MILK BISCUIT

One quart flour, 2-3 tsp. soda, 1 tsp. baking powder, 1-2 tsp. salt, sift together. Add 2 tbsp. melted lard in enough sour milk, beat until smooth, to make right, to knead lightly, bake quickly.

Mrs. A. M. Edsell

HEALTH BREAD

One half cup brown or white sugar, 1-4 cup melted butter, 1 tsp. soda, 2 tsp. salt, 1-4 cup Karo, 1 cup sour milk, 2 cups bran, 1-2 cup flour or graham flour, (or more) 1-4 cup raisins, 4 tbsp. cocoa. Mix dry ingredients and milk. Add Karo, stir well. Add butter last. Bake in moderate oven in iron skillet, good for infants and children.

Mrs. L. W. Grigsby

ORANGE BREAD OR ROLLS

One half cup yeast or 1-4 cup of water and 1 yeast cake, 1 egg well beaten, 1 tbsp. butter, 1 tbsp. crisco, 1 tsp. salt, 2 tbsp. sugar, grated rind of 2 oranges, 1-2 cup orange juice, 3 cups flour. Mix all till light and spongy Let rise and mix into loaf or rolls. This makes 1 loaf or 12 rolls.

———x———

CAKES

CHOCOLATE NUT FUDGE CAKE

Two cups sugar, 2-3 cup butter, 3 egg yolks, 1 cup sour milk,, 1-2 cup hot water, 1 tsp vanilla, 1 tsp. soda, 2 1-2 cups flour, 1 tsp baking powder, 1-2 cup cocoa, 1 cup nuts, whites of eggs added last.

ICING

One and one half cups powdered sugar, 1-3 cup butter, 2 tsp cocoa, white of 1 egg, stirred together and put on cake while it is hot.

Glenna Smith Burhans

WHITE CAKE

One and three quarters cups sugar sifted 3 times, 1-2 cup butter creamed, with sugar, 1 cup cold water, 2 cups flour sifted 3 times with 2 tsp. baking powder. Whites of 2 eggs beaten stiff and added last.

Nellie C. McMurray

CHOCOLATE STONE CAKE

One and one half cups sugar, 1-2 cup butter, 1 sq. chocolate in 5 tbsp. hot water, 3 egg yolks, 1-2 cup milk, 1 3-4 cup flour, 1 tsp. baking powder, whites folded in last. Bake in layers.

Mrs. Pete Bebernes

EGYPTIAN CAKE

Five tbsp. chocolate dissolved in 4 tbsp. boiling water, 1 1-2 cup sugar, 1-2 cup butter, 1-2 cup milk, 1 cup for larger cake, 4 eggs beaten separately, add whites last, 1 3-4 cups flour, 1 heaping tsp. baking powder, 1 tsp vanilla.

ICING

One and one half cups sugar, 1-2 cup hot water. Boil till it spins a good thread, add a piece of butter and let stand until cool. Add vanilla and beat until creamy.

Mrs. William E. Quinn

GINGER BREAD

One cup butter, 1 cup sugar, 1 cup molasses, 3 cups flour, 1 egg, 2 tsp soda dissolved in a litte warm water, 1 level tbsp ginger and spices to taste. Beat butter, sugar, add molasses, soda, spices and yolk of egg, and beat. Add flour and egg white, then water and beat well.

Mrs. Wm. Lewis

MOCHA CAKE

Two heaping tbsp butter, 1 1-2 cups sugar, 2 eggs, 1 1-2 cups milk, 1-4 tsp salt, 1 tsp flour, 3 tsp baking powder, 4 tbsp chocolate. Cream butter and sugar, add yolks of eggs well beaten, add milk, salt, flavoring and chocolate. Mix well and add beaten whites. Bake in 3 layers in a moderate oven.

Mrs. Nels Jensen

PRUNE CAKE

Two eggs, 1 cup sugar, 1-2 cup oil, 1 tbsp chocolate, 1-2 tsp each of nutmeg and cloves, 1 tsp soda in 1-2 cup prune juice, 1 1-2 cup flour, 1 cup prunes put through food chopper.

Mrs. William E Quinn

2 cups flour

FRUIT CAKE

Two cups brown sugar, 1 cup molasses, 4 eggs, 1 cup butter or 3-4 cup oil, 1 cup milk, 5 cups sifted flour, 2 tsp baking powder, 1 tsp soda dissolved in warm water and added to molasses, 1 tbsp cinnamon, 2 tsp nutmeg, 2 lbs. raisins, 1 cup nuts, 1 tsp of lemon and vanilla.

2 EGG FRUIT CAKE

One pound brown sugar, 1 pound raisins, 1 pound currants, 4 cups of flour, 1 cup butter, 1 cup milk, 1-2 cup nuts chopped, 2 eggs, 1-4 pound citron, 1-2 cup molasses, if white sugar is used put in 1 cup molasses, 1-2 tsp nutmeg, allspice, cloves, a rounding tsp baking powder.

Glenna Smith Burhans

SPONGE DROPS

Beat light 3 eggs and put in a cup of sugar. Stir in 1 heaping cup of flour, sifted with 1 tsp. cream of tartar and 1-2 tsp soda. Flavor with lemon. Butter tin sheets and drop mixture in teaspoonsful about 3 inches apart. Watch very closely in oven to prevent burning.

Mrs. Nels Jensen

EGGLESS CHOCOLATE CAKE

One and one half cup brown or white sugar, 1-2 cup chocolate, 2 1-2 cups flour, 1 tsp baking powder, 1-2 tsp salt, 1 tsp vanilla, 1-2 cup butter or oil, lard, 1 cup hot water, 1 tsp soda, 1 cup buttermilk. Cream sugar and shortening. Add chocolate dissolved in 1-2 water. Then soda in other half. Beat in sour milk and vanilla. Bake in layers or loaf.

Mrs. Nellie McMurray

INEXPENSIVE SPONGE CAKE

Beat 2 eggs and 1 cup sugar and a inch of salt, until as creamy as can be made. Add 1 cup flour sifted with 1 tsp baking powder. Moisten with 13 tsp cold water and 1 tsp of any kind of flavoring.

Mrs. Nels Jensen

APPLE SAUCE CAKE

One cup sugar, 2 cups flour, 3 tbsp chocolate, 2 tsp soda, 1 tsp nutmeg, 2 tsp cloves, 1-2 tsp nutmeg, 1 tbsp cornstarch. Sift these all together and add 1 cup chopped raisins, 1 cup chopped nuts, 1 1-2 cups cold apple sauce and 1-2 cup melted butter.

Bake in shallow pan.

Mrs. Wm. Lewis

DATE CAKE

Three quarters cup butter, 1 1-2 cup sugar, cup chopped nuts, 1 pound of dates, 1 pound of raisins, 2 tbsp citron, 1 tbsp orange peel chopped, 2 3-4 cups flour, 1 tsp soda in 1 cup boiling water. Bake in slow oven 1 hour.

Mrs. Sam Lyons Jr.

PLAIN LAYER CAKE

One half cup shortening, 1 1-2 cup sugar, 1-2 cup milk, 3 cups flour, 1-4 tsp salt, 1-2 cup water, 1 tsp vanilla, 2 egg whites beaten stiff, 3 tsp baking powder. Cream butter and 1 cup sugar, gradually add the other 1-2 cup sugar with a little milk. Sift flour, baking powder and salt, and add alternately to first mixture with milk and water. Beat in flavoring and egg whites. This makes 3 layers.

Mrs. Wm. Lewis

HOT WATER CAKE

Beat 4 eggs light, 1 white may be saved for icing if desired. Add 1 1-2 cup sugar and beat. To this add 2 cups flour and then 1 cup hot water. Add slowly beating all the while. Lastly add 2 tsp baking powder and 1 tsp flavoring and bake.

Mrs. Nellie McMurray

CREAM VELVET CAKE

One and one fourth cups sifted flour, 1 tsp vanilla, 1-2 tsp lemon extract, 1-4 tsp salt, 1-3 cup vegetable oil or cream, 2-3 cup water, 3-4 cup sugar, 2 eggs. Sift dry ingredients together. Mix oil and flavoring and add to dry mixture. Drop in egg yolks and beat. Then fold in whites beaten stiff. Two layers.

Mrs. Nellie McMurray

WALNUT MAPLE CAKE

Cream 1-3 cup butter, 1 cup brown sugar, yolks of 3 eggs and 1-2 cup milk. Sift and add to above 1 1-3 cup flour, 2 tsp baking powder, 1-4 tsp salt and beat. To this add 1 cup ground walnuts, whites of 2 eggs and 1 tsp vanilla. Bake in angel cake tin.

Mrs Wm. Lewis

BURNT SUGAR CAKE

One half cup butter, 1 1-2 cup of

sugar, 3 egg yolks added 1 at a time, 1 cup cold water, 1 tsp vanilla, 2 cups flour. Beat 5 minutes. Then add 2 tbsp burnt sugar, 2 rounding tsp baking powder in 1-2 cup flour, beat whites of eggs slightly and add.

Burnt Sugar

Put 1 cup sugar in a skillet heat until it is all brown, and syrupy, then add 2-3 cup either hot or cold water, and stir until dissolved.

Glenna Smith Burhans

JELLY ROLL

One cup sugar, 1 cup sifted flour, 4 eggs, 1 tsp cream of tartar, 1-2 tsp soda, pinch of salt. Bake in large square pan. When done spread with jelly and roll.

Mrs. Pete Bebernes

EGGLESS CAKE

One cup sugar, 1-2 cup butter, 1 cup sour milk, 1 tsp salt, 1 tsp soda, cinnamon and cloves, 1-2 tsp ginger, 2 1-2 cups flour.

Mrs. Pete Bebernes

ANGEL CAKE

Whites of 11 eggs, 1 1-2 cups of granulated sugar sifted twice, 1 cup flour sifted with 1 tsp cream of tartar 4 times. 1 tsp vanilla. Bake in an ungreased pan 40 minutes. When done invert pan on two cups and let stand until cake is cold.

Mrs. Jos. B. Miller

BIRTHDAY CAKE

One cup butter, 2 cups sugar, 3 cups flour with 1 tsp cream of tartar in it. Four eggs, yolks and whites beaten separately, 1-2 cup milk with 1-2 tsp soda dissolved in it, 1 saltspoon mace, grated rind of half an orange, 1 tsp vanilla. Ice with white icing.

Mrs. Jos. B. Miller

APPLE SAUCE CAKE

One cup sugar, 1-2 cup butter, 1 tsp salt, 1-2 tsp cloves, 1 tsp cinnamon, 1 cup raisins, 1 cup walnuts, 1 tsp soda dissolved in a little warm water then stir into 1 cup of unsweetened apple sauce, add this and beat thoroughly adding 2 heaping cups flour, bake 45 minutes.

Virginia Ontiveros

SPONGE CAKE

Measure and combine 1 1-4 cups

sugar, 1 cup water, place over slow fire until sugar dissolves, then boil until it spins a thread. Beat 6 egg whites very stiff; pour syrup over them beating constantly until quite cool. Beat yolks until thick and lemon colored, add 1 tsp vanilla. Beat, then pour in the white mixture, measure and sift 1 cup flour, 1-4 tsp salt, 1 tsp cream of tartar. Fold into egg mixture and bake in a loaf, when done invert pan, allow a circulation of air under cake and when shrunk sufficiently lift off the pan.

CALIFORNIA CAKE

One cup granulated sugar, 1 cup brown sugar, 1 cup shortening, 1 cup water, 1 cup walnuts, 1 cup seeded raisins, 2 tsp cinnamon, 1 tsp soda, 2 1-2 cups flour. Boil sugar, shortening, raisins, cinnamon and water 5 minutes and let cool. Add soda dissolved in a little boiling water, add flour, then walnuts. Bake in loaf 1 hour.

Mrs. Toynette Wilson

DEVILS FOOD CAKE

One half cup butter, 1 cup brown sugar, 1-2 cup white sugar, creamed together, add 2 egg yolks beaten stiff, 1-2 cup ground chocolate dissolved in 1-2 cup boiling coffee, 1-2 cup buttermilk in which dissolve 1 tsp soda. Sift together and add 2 heaping cups flour and 1 tsp baking powder, then 2 egg whites whipped stiff, and 1 tsp vanilla. Bake in a moderate oven. Makes 3 layers. Use white icing.

Mrs. W. A. Barrett

JELLY ROLL

Three eggs, 1 cup sugar, 3 tbsp cold water, 1-2 tsp salt, 1 tsp baking powder, 1 cup flour, jelly or jam. Beat eggs and sugar until thick, add water, then flour, salt, baking powder. Line a shallow pan with oil paper. Pour in and bake in quick oven. Turn on cloth sprinkled with sugar spread with jelly and roll.

Mrs M. P. Hourihan

NEVER FAIL CAKE

Sift together 1 1-2 cups flour, 1 cup sugar and 2 level tsp baking powder, a pinch of salt. Use the same cup, break into it 2 or 3 eggs and fill cup to top with heavy sweet cream. Beat up with a fork, pour into bowl and add flour. Bake as loaf or layer cake.

D. E. B.

FRUIT CAKE

....One pound sugar, 1 pound flour, 1 pound butter, 9 eggs, 3 pounds of currants, 2 pounds of raisins, 1 oz. citron, 1 oz. mace, 1 oz. nutmeg, 1 1-2 oz. cinnamon, 1 tsp cloves, 1 tsp ginger, 1 1-2 wine glasses of brandy.

Mrs. William Anderson

SOFT GINGER BREAD

One half cup sugar, 1 cup molasses, 1-2 cup butter, tsp each ginger, cinnamon and cloves, 2 tsp soda dissolved in cup of boiling water, 2 1-2 cups flour, add 2 well beaten eggs last thing before cooking. Bake 1-2 hour in very slow oven.

Mrs. F. M. Kilmer Jr.

SNOW BALLS

Any good white cake baked about 1 inch or less thick. Cut into cubes and have ready a bowl of grated fresh cocoanut and one of boiled icing. Quickly dip each cube first in the icing and then in the cocoanut until heavily covered.

Mrs. F. M. Kilmer, Jr.

MOLASSES CAKE

Sift together the following: 2 and 1-2 cups flour, 2 tsp soda, 2 tsp of ginger 1 1-2 tsp cinnamon, 1-2 tsp cloves, 1-2 tsp nutmeg, 1-2 tsp baking powder. Mix 3 beaten egg yolks and 1 egg white with 2-3 cup sugar, then add 3-4 cup molasses, and 1-2 cup salad oil. Add dry ingredients and lastly add 1 cup of strong coffee. Bake in large shallow pan.

Filling

Cut cake in 2 equal parts, and spread quickly over the cake icing made as follows: 2 cups sugar, 1-2 cup water, 1-4 tsp salt, 1 tbsp Karo boiled until it spins a thread. Pour this over stiffly beaten egg whites and beat rather thick. Place in pan of hot water to keep soft and then spread.

Mrs. C. V. Barker

BANANA CAKE

One and one half cups sugar,, 2-3 cup butter, 1 cup mashed bananas, 1 cup walnuts. 1 tsp soda, 4 tbsp sour milk, 2 eggs, 1 1-2 cups flour. Cream butter and sugar. Add beaten eggs, mix well. Add soda to sour milk and add alternately with flour, add bananas and nuts and bake in loaf for 45 minutes.

Agnes Potter

ALMOND CAKE

One pound granulated sugar, 1-4 pound ground almonds, 2 cups bread crumbs, 1 tsp cinnamon, 1-4 tsp of cloves, 2 tbsp fruit juice, 8 eggs, 2 heaping tsp baking powder, 1 tsp allspice. Beat yolks of eggs and the sugar Add spices and nuts, baking powder, crumbs. Add well beaten whites of eggs. Bake in three equal layers and put together with milk frosting.

DEVILS CAKE—MOCHA FILLING
Custard Part

One cup grated bitter chocolate, 1 cup brown sugar, 1-2 cup sweet milk, yolk of 1 egg, 1 tsp vanilla. Stir together in sauce pan, cook slowly and set away to cool.

For Cake

One cup brown sugar, 1-2 cup butter, 2 cups flour, 1-2 cup sweet milk, 2 eggs. Cream butter, sugar, yolks of eggs and add milk, sifted flour and whites of eggs, beaten stiff, beat thoroughly and stir in custard. Last add 1 tsp of soda dissolved in little warm water.

Mocha Filling

Three large cups powdered sugar free from lumps, 1 heaping tbsp of butter creamed into the sugar, yolk of 1 egg, 4 tbsp ground chocolate moistened with cold black coffee. Add chopped walnuts, dates and raisins and flavor with vanilla.

Mrs F. M. Kilmer Jr.

UPSIDE DOWN CAKE

Put 1 1-2 cups half whites, half brown sugar into an iron skillet with 3 heaping tbsp of butter. Melt and mix thoroughly. Arrange sliced pineapple on this, set aside to cool.

Batter

One cup flour, 1 cup sugar, 3 eggs beaten separately, 3 tsp baking powder, 7 tbsp of pineapple juice. Pour over sugar and pineapple in skillet, bake half hour. Upset. Serve with whipped cream.

Mrs F. M. Kilmer Jr.

LIBERTY COFFEE CAKE

Three cups flour, 1-2 tsp salt, 3 tbsp sugar, 2 tsp baking powder, 2 beaten eggs, 2-3 cup milk, 2 tbsp melted butter. Spread in buttered pan.

Top Dressing

Two tbsp flour, 4 tbsp sugar, 1 tbsp cinnamon, 2 tbsp butter. Cream together and spread on top of cake in pan and bake in hot oven until done.

Mrs .Frank Torrence

WHITE LAYER CAKE

Whites of 6 eggs beaten stiff. Cream together until very smooth 2 cups sugar and 1 cup butter. To this add 1 cup milk and 1 tsp vanilla extract. After sifting flour, measure 3 level cups. Sift again with 1 heaping tsp baking powder. Last add beaten egg whites This makes a large 3 layer cake or can be baked in loaf.

Mrs F. M. Kilmer Jr.

WHITE FRUIT CAKE

One cup butter, 2 cups sugar, 1 cup sweet milk, 2 1-2 cups flour, 2 tsp baking powder, 1 pound each of raisins, figs anl blanched almonds, 1-4 pound citron all chopped fine. One tsp lemon extract. Mix all together before adding the fruits the following: put baking powder in the flour, mix it well before adding to the other ingredients, sift a little flour over the fruit before stirring it in. Bake slowly 2 hours and test with a splint. A cup of cocoanut is a nice addition to this cake.

Mrs. Margaret Hourihan

SOUR CREAM CAKE

Two cups sugar and 1 egg beaten thoroughly, add a little salt, 1 cup sour cream, 1 scant tsp soda, 1 tsp cloves or chocolate, vanilla, 1 cup flour. Mix as usual, bake in moderate oven.

Virginia Ontiveros

SAME OLD CAKE

One cup sugar, 1 egg 2 1-2 cups flour, 4 tbsp milk, 1 cup warm waterø 4 level tsp baking powder, flavor and add 1-2 scant cup butter. Add sugar and egg well beaten to shortening, put milk in cup, fill with warm water. Add flour and baking powder sifted together, beat and add flavoring. Bake in moderate oven. Omit the last 1-2 cup flour and add several spoons of cocoa to make a delicious dark cake, then use boiled frosting. For a marble cake, reserve part of batter and add enough cocoa to darken 1-2 of it. Bake in loaf and ice, as desired. Add your favorite nuts to make a nut cake. By adding a little more flour, it makes nice drop cakes.

Mrs. Katherine M. Hill

STRAWBERRY CAKE

One cup sugar, 4 tbsp shortening, 1 egg, 2 cups flour, 3 tsp baking powder, 1-8 tsp salt, 1 cup milk, 1 tsp vanilla extract, 1-2 pint heavy cream, 1 quart strawberries.

Cream sugar and shortening, add beaten egg, add part of flour, baking powder and salt, which have been sifted together, then part of the milk, mix well and add remainder of flour, mix in remainder of the milk and flavoring. Bake in shallow greased pans in moderate oven for 20 or 30 minutes. When cold split in half and spread whipped cream and crushed sweetened strawberries between layers. Cover top with whipped cream and whole berries.

Mrs. M. F. McGee

SPICE CAKE

One half cup shortening, 1 1-3 cup brown sugar, 2 eggs well beaten without separating, 2 cups flour sifted with 3 tsp baking powder, 1 tsp cinnamon, 1-2 tsp nutmeg, 1-4 tsp of cloves, 1-4 tsp allspice, 1 tsp vanilla, 1-2 cup cold coffee. Sift flour with spices and baking powder. Cream shortening, add sugar gradually, and beat well, add beaten eggs, then alternately the flour and coffee. Add flavoring and bake in layers or loaf in moderate oven. Raisins may be added if baked in loaf.

Mrs. William J. Phelps Jr.

PRUNE CAKE

Cream together 1 1-2 cups sugar and 1 tbsp butter, add 4 well beaten egg yolks, 1 1-2 cup prunes run through colander, dissolve 1 tsp of soda in prunes. Sift together and add 2 1-2 cups flour, 1 tsp baking powder, 1 tsp cinnamon, 1-2 tsp each of cloves and allspice. Add 2 tbsp chocolate dissolved in a little hot water, then 2 egg whites whipped stiff. Use 2 other whites for filling. Bake in layers.

Filling and Icing for Prune Cake
Two and one half cups sugar, 1-2
cup light Karo syrup, 1-2 cup water,
boil until it spins a thread. Take off
stove and pour slowly over 2 egg
whites beaten stiff. Beat constantly
and when it begins to thicken add
1 1-2 tsp vanilla, and beat until the
right consistency to spread.
Mrs. W. A. Barrett

SPONGE CAKES
Beat 4 egg yolks stiff and add 3
tbsp cold water and beat until thick
and lemon colored. Add 1 cup of
sugar gradually. Put 1 1-2 tbsp corn
starch in cup and fill cup with flour.
Mix and sift with 1 1-4 tsp baking
powder and pinch of salt. Add then
4 egg whites whipped stiff. Flavor
with 1 tsp lemon extract. Bake in
loaf 30 minutes in moderate oven.
Mrs. T. F. Spalding

JAM CAKE
Cream 1 cup sugar and 3-4 cup of
butter, add 3 eggs and beat well, dissolve 1 tsp soda in 2 tbsp sour milk.
Add this and 2 1-2 cups flour, then
1 tsp cinnamon, 1-2 tsp each of cloves and nutmeg and last 1 large cup
blackberry jam. Bake in 2 layers
and use white icing.
Mrs. H. T. Stark

POOR MAN'S ANGEL CAKE
Whites of 4 eggs slightly beaten,
add pinch of salt and 1-4 tsp cream
of tartar and then beat until stiff.
Then beat in 5-8 cup sifted sugar, 1
tbsp at time, when sugar is used
then beat in 1-2 cup flour sifted 4
times. 1 tbsp at a time until all of
flour is used. Bake in ungreased
pan in a slow oven about 40 minutes.
Mrs. C. R. Weston

MOCHA CAKE
One and one half cups sugar, 1-2
cup shortening, 1-2 cup black coffee,
2 cups flour, 1 cup chocolate, 1 tsp
soda, 3-4 cup boiling water, 2 eggs.
Cream sugar and shortening, add
eggs, coffee with soda in, sift the
and add to mixture, then add chocolate. Last add boiling water.
Ione Jamison

3 EGG CAKE
Cream together 2 cups sugar and
1-2 cup butter, add 3 egg yolks
beaten stiff, 1-4 tsp salt, 1 cup sweet
milk, 2 tsp baking powder, flour to
make a thin batter, lastly the 3 egg
whites beaten stiff, flavor and bake
in layers.
Mrs. T. F. Spalding

DATE CAKE
Pour 1 cup hot water over 1 cup
dates and let stand a few minutes.
Cream togther 1 cup sugar and 1
tbsp butter, add 1 well beaten egg,
add dates and 1-2 cup chopped nuts.
Sift together and add 1 1-4 cup of
flour and 1 tsp soda mixed. Bake
in loaf.
Mrs. W. A. Barrett

JELLY CAKE
One cup sugar 1 1-2 cup flour, 3
tsp baking powder, 1 egg, 6 tbsp
hot water, bake in slow oven, put in
cloth until cold so as to keep in
shape. Roll with any kind of jelly.
Virginia Ontiveros

POTATO CAKE
Two cups white sugar, 1 cup butter, 1 cup hot mashed potatoes, 1-2
cup sweet milk, 4 egg yolks beaten
stiff, 5 tsp chocolate melted in 1-4
cup hot coffee, 1 scant tbsp cloves,
1 heaping tbsp each of cinnamon
and nutmeg, 1 cup chopped walnuts,
2 cups flour, 2 tsp baking powder, 4
egg whites beaten stiff. Mix in the
order given and bake in 4 layers
using the following filling:
Filling
Melt 1 1-2 square chocolate in 1
cup hot milk, take 2 level tsp flour
wet with cold milk, add to the hot
milk and cook until thick. Pour
over 2 well beaten eggs and 5 tbsp
sugar, add 1 tsp vanilla and 6 marshmallows. Spread between layers and
on top of cake.
Mrs. T. F. Spalding

LOAF CAKE
Three fourths cup butter, 3 cups
flour, 3 eggs well beaten, 1 cup milk,
1 cup sugar, flavoring to taste, 2 tsp
baking powder. Beat all well.
Mrs. Wm. Step

LAYER CAKE
One cup milk, 1 cup sugar, 2 1-2
cups flour, 3 tbsp melted butter, 3
eggs, 2 heaping tsp baking powder.
Beat well and bake in 4 layers. Add
flavoring.
Filling
Put in double boiler 1 pint milk.

When hot add 1 cup sugar, 2 well beaten egg, 2 tbsp butter, thicken by adding corn starch. Flavor to taste.

Mrs. Wm. Step

CHEESE CAKE

One and one half pound cottage cheese, 1 cup sugar, 4 eggs, 1-2 pint cream, few grains of salt, 1-2 lemon (juice and rind) 1-4 tsp vanilla, 1-4 cup flour, 1 package sweiback, (6 oz) 1 cup sugar, 1 tsp cinnamon, 1-2 cup melted butter, 1-2 cup walnuts. Roll sweiback fine, mix with 1 cup sugar, cinnamon, chopped nuts and melted butter. Set aside 1 cup of this mixture to sprinkle over top. Butter well a 9 inch spring form, spread and press sweiback mixture on bottom and sides of form. Beat eggs without separating, with sugar until light Add salt, lemon and the vanilla. Add cream gradully, then cheese and flour. Blend all together and strain and mash through fine sieve. Stir until uniform, pour in the form lined with sweiback, and sprinkle remaining sweiback mixture on top. Bake at 350 degrees 1 hour. Let stand in oven, door open to cool and when nearly cold remove from oven.

Mrs. C. M. Jones

RIBBON CAKE

One half cup butter, 4 eggs, 2 cups sugar, 3 cups flour, 1 tsp chocolate, 3 rounding tsp of baking powder, 1 cup milk, 1 tsp vanilla extract, 1 tsp lemon or orange extract, 10 drops fruit coloring. Beat the butter to a cream, add sugar and yolks of eggs and beat thoroughly. Sift the baking powder and flour togther and add them alternately with the milk. Beat the whites of eggs to a stiff froth and stir them carefully into the other ingredients. Separate the mixture into thirds: to one third add the melted chocoate which has been dissolved over hot water, and the orange extract; to another third, the lemon extract and fruit coloring to the last third add vanilla extract, bake in layer pans of the same size in moderate oven for 30 minutes. When done turn out. Cool and spread each layer with soft icing. Place one of the pans on top layer with weights, let these stand one hour, then remove pan and ice top and decorate.

Mrs. C. M. Jones

FRUIT CAKE

One half pound Cottolene. 1 lb. brown sugar, rolled, yolks of 12 eggs, 2 cups molasses, 1 lb, flour, 1 tbsp cinnamon, 1 tsp each of cloves, allspice nutmeg, ginger, salt and soda, 2 1-2 lbs seeded raisins. 2 lbs currants, 1-2 lb citron chopped, 1-4 lb candied orange peel, 1-2 cup brandy, Add egg whites last. Bake in moderate oven.

Mrs. Wm. Step

BANANA CAKE

One and a half cups sugar, 1 cup thick sour cream, sweetened with soda, 1 cup mashed ripe bananas, 1 cup nut meats, 1 tsp soda, 4 tbsp sour milk, 2 eggs, 2 1-2 cups flour, bake in loaf.

Mrs. C. O. Gardner

✗ TAFT CAKE

Sift together 1 cup sugar, 4 cup flour, 2 level tsp soda, 1-2 tsp each of cloves, cinnamon and nutmeg, 1 tbsp corn starch, 3 tbsp chocolate. Mix together 1-2 cup melted butter, 1 1-2 cups apple sauce, 1 cup chopped nuts, 1 cup raisins, combine the two mixtures and bake 1 hour.

Mrs. Sam Lyons Jr.

BLACKBERRY CAKE

Cream 1 cup sugar, 1-2 cup butter, yolks of 3 eggs, 2 cups flour, 3 tbsp blackberry juice, 1 scant tsp each of cloves, cinnamon, allspice. Then mix 1 tsp soda with a little flour. When all are well mixed add the beaten whites of 3 eggs.

Frosting

Three cups powdered sugar mixed with blackberry juice to right consistency, 2 cups granulated sugar, 8 tbsp cold water. Boil until it spins thread. 8 tbsp cold water in package Knox gelatine. fix this first, then pour syrup slowly into gelatine, also powdered sugar and juice, then beat, when thickened put in 1-4 tsp salt and flavor.

Mrs C. M. Jones

WHITE CAKE

Cream 1-2 cup butter, add gradually 1 cup sugar, sift together 2 scant cups flour and 4 level tsp baking powder and a pinch of salt. . Add this alternately to the first mixture with 1-2 cup milk. Lastly add 4 egg whites which have been beaten stiff and bake in layers or loaf.

Mrs. A. H. Barth

TROPICAL FRUIT CAKE

One fourth cup butter 1-2 cup of brown sugar, 1 cup white sugar, 3 eggs, 1-4 cup buttermilk or sour milk, 1 sq. bitter chocolate melted over hot water, 1 cup grated pineapple, 1 large banana mashed, 12 large dates chopped 1-2 cup walnuts, 2 cups of flour 1 level tsp soda, 1-2 tsp cream of tartar. Sift dry ingredients 3 times. Cream butter with brown sugar, add white sugar alternately with milk add eggs, one at a time, beat well. Add chocolate, fruits and flavor. Bake 45 minutes.

Agnes Potter

HONEY CAKES

One large cup sugar, 1 large cup honey, 6 tbsp grated chocolate. Let all this melt. When cool add 4 eggs, 2 tbsp cinnamon, 3 cups flour, 1 tsp baking powder. Cook in shallow pan and cut in small squares.

Mrs. John Forbes

COFFEE CAKE

One cup brown sugar, 1 cup of butter, 2 eggs, 1-2 cup molasses, 1 cup strong coffee 1-2 tsp soda dissolved in molasses, 1 tsp cloves, 2 tsp cinnamon, 1-4 tsp salt, 1 cup of chopped nuts, 1 cup raisins, 4 cups flour, 2 tsp baking powder. Mix and bake.

Mrs. Frank Fitzgerald

THREE LAYER WHITE CAKE

Five egg whites, 2 cups sugar, 1 scant cup butter or crisco, 1 cup of milk, 3 tsp baking powder, 3 cup sifted flour, 1-2 tsp almond flavoring. Cream sugar and butter, beat whites stiff, sift flour, pinch of salt and the baking powder together. Add the dry ingredients alternately with the milk to the creamed butter and the sugar and fold in the beaten whites. While this is baking prepare the filling.

Filling

Six egg yolks, the sixth white save for frosting. 1 cup thick sour cream, 1 cup sugar, cook over very slow fire until thick. Add 1 cup chopped almonds and spread between the 3 layers. Cover top and sides with a frosting.

Frosting

One cup sugar, 1-3 cup water. Add pinch of cream of tartar. Boil until it makes a firm ball when tested in cold water. Turn it over the stiffly beaten egg while beating contantly until it is cold and thick. Add almond flavoring and spread on cake. Dot top with almonds cut in half.

POTATO CAKE

One cup butter, 2 cups sugar, 1-3 cup sweet milk, 2 cups sifted flour, 1 cup mashed cold potatoes, 1 cup chopped nuts, 4 eggs, 4 tbsp grated chocolate, 1 tsp each of cloves, cinnamon, nutmeg, 2 tsp baking powder. Bake in moderate oven, fruit may be added if desired, such as jams or grated pineapple or cherries.

Mae Means

VELVET SPONGE CAKE

Four eggs beaten separately, the yolks first, add 1 cup sugar, when sugar is mixed in, beat about 5 minutes, then add 3 tbsp corn starch in a measuring cup and fill cup with flour, 1 1-2 tsp of baking powder, a pinch of salt sifted with flour, 1 tbsp lemon extract. Last fold in the beaten whites. Bake in an ungreased cake tin in a moderate oven for 40 minutes.

Mrs. Fernie Jamison

BOSTON CAKE

One pound flour, 1 pound sugar, 1-2 pound of butter, 1 cup of sour cream, 5 eggs, 1 tsp soda, 1-8 tsp each of cinnamon, nutmeg and cloves. Cream butter and sugar, then add well beaten yolks of eggs. Dissolve the soda in cream and add the flour alternately with whites of eggs beaten stiff. Add spices. Fruit can be added. Bake in moderately hot oven, especially if fruit is added.

Emma Ellen Donahue

ANGEL SPONGE

One and one fourth cups, or 9 to 11 egg whites 1 cup and 2 tbsp of sugar, 1-2 tsp salt, 1 tsp cream of tartar, 6 egg yolks, 1-2 cups S. D. cake flour.

White Part

One half tsp vanilla to white part. 2-3 cup flour to yellow part 1-2 tsp orange extract to yellow part. Put egg whites on large platter, beat until foamy, add salt and cream of tartar, beat till stiff but not dry.

Fold in sugar. Divide mixture in 2 parts. To one part carefully fold in 1-2 cup flour and vanilla. To the other part 6 beaten egg yolks, 2-3 cups flour and orange extract.

Mrs. Lang

POTATO CAKE

Two cups sugar, 1 cup butter, 1-2 cup sweet milk, 1 cup chopped walnuts, 2 cups flour, 1 cup mashed potatoes, warm, 1-2 cup chocolate dissolved in warm water, 2 tsp baking powder 4 eggs well beaten 1 tsp of cinnamon, cloves, nutmeg and vanilla, 1 cup pineapple, 1 cup cherries.

Mrs. Otha Williams

FRUIT CAKE

One half pound butter, 1-2 pound flour, (2 cups) 2 cups brown sugar, 1 small bottle cherries, 1 cup figs, 3 pounds raisins, 1-2 pound each of butternuts, walnuts, almonds, chopped coarse, 1 cup pineapple, 1-2 cup of any preserves, 5 eggs, 1-2 cup of brandy, 1 tsp cloves, cinnamon, nutmeg and mace and 2 tsp baking powder.

DEVIL FOOD CAKE

Two cups sugar, 1-2 cup shortening, 1-2 cup cold coffee, 2 cups flour, 1 cup chocolate, 1 tsp soda, cinnamon, allspice and cloves, 3 eggs, 1 cup boiling coffee or water. Cream sugar and shortening, add eggs and beat hard. Add cold coffee and soda and add flour and chocolate and the spices and beat hard. At last add the boiling water and bake in 3 layers and put together with white icing.

Mrs. Lang

PRUNE CAKE

One half cup butter 1 cup sugar, 2 eggs, 3-4 cup sour milk, 1 1-2 cup flour, 1 tsp soda, 3 tsp chocolate, 1-2 tsp cinnamon, 1-8 tsp cloves, 1-4 tsp alspice, 1 cup chopped prunes, 2 cups chopped nuts.

Mrs. Lang

SOUR CREAM CAKE

Beat 2 eggs until light add 1 cup sugar slowly to eggs, beating all the time. Take 1 1-2 cups flous, 1-2 tsp soda, 1-4 tsp salt, 1 tsp nutmeg, 1-2 tsp allspice, and 1-2 tsp cinnamon and add to eggs alternately with 1 cup sour cream.

Mrs. Lang

———————X———————

CONFECTIONS

FONDANT

Two and one half cups sugar, 1-3 cup corn syrup, 1 cup water. Cook until soft ball is formed in water, Remove, cool until white ,flavor and drop on waxed paper. If it gets too hard set in pan of hot water.

Glenna Smith Buhans

POTATO CANDY

Bake a medium size potato, take out of shell and mash and beat real light. Add confectionery sugar until it will hold its shape, flavor and divide in 3 portions, color one pink, one dark with melted chocolate and leave one white. Place in layers, let set and cut in squares or roll as a jelly roll and after it sets an hour cut in thin slices.

Mrs. W. A. Barrett

PANOCHE

Three cups sugar, 1-2 cup corn syrup, 1-2 cup cream. Boil slowly until it forms a hard ball in cold water. Let cool just a little and stir until creamy. Add 1 tsp vanilla before stirring, also add 1 cup walnuts.

Glenna Smith Burhans

CREAM CARAMELS

Put 1 cup sugar, 1-2 cup white karo and 1-2 cup sweet cream in a sauce pan and stir until dissolved, then boil slowly until it forms a soft ball when tested. Then stir gently and do not beat or it will become grainy. Add another 1-2 cup cream and boil until it makes a soft ball when tested, then add another 1-2 cup cream and boil until it makes a rather firm ball when tested in cold water, then pour in buttered plates. When cold cut in squares and wrap in wax paper.

Mrs. Frank Fitzgerald

ORIENTAL DELIGHTS

Take equal weights of dates, stoned, figs, raisins and prunes, and put through meat chopper. Mold and roll thin using powdered sugar to keep from sticking to board. Cut out with small cookie cutter and dust with powdered sugar. Keep for a few days before serving. A cup of nut meats ground with the fruit adds to its flavor and food value.

Mrs. James A. Westcott

COCOANUT FUDGE

Boil together 3 cups sugar, 1 cup cream, 1 cup karo, butter size of wa'nut until it forms a soft ball when tested in water. Take off and flavor with vanilla and add 1 box of shredded cocoanut, beat till creamy. Pour in buttered plates and mark in squares before cold.

Mrs. T. F. Spalding

POPCORN BALLS

Pop 3 pounds of shelled popcorn. Remove corn that has not popped, and mix 1 pound granulated sugar 1 pint syrup and 1-2 pint water, and stir until sugar is dissolved. Cook until sugar thermometer registers 240 degress. Add 1-2 oz. butter and cook to 242 degrees. Pour a little of the syrup over the freshly popped corn and mold into balls. Add more syrup and mold a few more until all the corn is used. This amount should make about 40 balls.

Mrs. Jos. B Miller

BUTTER SCOTCH

One cup karo syrup, 1 cup sugar, 1-2 cup butter, 2 tbsp vinegar, pinch of soda. Boil until it forms hard ball when dipped in water.

Cecelia Minetti

MAINE BUTTERSCOTCH

Two cups granulated sugar, 1-2 cup vinegar, 1-4 cup molasses, 1-2 cup of butter. Place over a low fire and stir constantly until the sugar is dissolved. Then continue to cook without stirring to 290 degrees or until the mixture forms a hard ball when tried in cold water. Meanwhile sprinkle 1 cup of shelled peanuts coarsely chopped in the bottom of a buttered pan and pour the candy mixture over the prepared pan. When slightly cool cut into small squares and when thoroughly cool break into squares and serve.

Theresa Costa

IMPERIAL FUDGE

Two cups granulated sugar 1 cup thin cream or rich milk. Place over a low flame until the sugar dissolves. Continue cooking without stirring until candy thermometer registers 238 degrees or until the mixture forms a soft ball in cold water. Remove from the heat place in a large bowl of cold water and let stand undisturbed until the outside of the candy dish feels cool to the hand. Remove the pan from the water at this point and add 1-8 tsp of salt, 1-4 tsp rose extract, 2 tbsp butter, 1 cup blanched almonds chopped fine, 1-2 cup of marshmallows cut into halves. Beat the mixture well until thoroughly blended, creamy and thick. Shape on a buttered plate. Allow to cool slightly and cut into desired shapes.

Theresa Costa

DIVINITY CANDY

Four cups of white sugar, 1 cup of karo syrup, 1 cup of hot water, 3 egg whites, 2 cups of chopped walnuts, also cut up crystalized fruit for extra nice. Stir sugar syrup and water before putting on to boil. Let it boil until it forms a good dry hair like string, then pour half of this slowly into the beaten whites of 3 eggs. Let remained cook until when dropped into small sauce dish you can hear it crackle. Now add to the first part, beating quickly, add nuts and vanilla flavoring. Keep on beating until the mixture when dropped from spoon does not sink in, then pour out quickly on platter or small deep pan slightly buttered. Use a large kettle for cooking, also large bowl for mixing.

Theresa Costa

CHOCOLATE FUDGE

Combine 2 cups granulated sugar, 1 cup milk, 2 squares chocolate, 1-2 tsp salt. Cook over slow fire stirring constantly using wooden spoon until the sugar is dissolved. Place candy thermometer in position in sauce pan and continue boiling gently without stirring until 230 degrees or soft ball may be handied by testing in glass of water, then remove from fire, set it in large bowl of cold water. Let pan stand undisturbed until no heat in fudge mixture, then remove from bowl of water and add 2 tbsp butter and 1-2 tsp vanilla. Begin to beat fudge gradually working in the butter. Continue beating, pushing spoon forward, lifting up the mixture, turning it over and bringing it back until it becomes creamy and thick. Then turn on buttered plate, shape with spatula 1 inch thick. Allow to cool slightly and cut into squares.

CANDIED ORANGE PEEL

Cut peel in narrow strips, cover with cold water and boil 20 minutes. Change water and boil again 20 minutes, change again and boil 20 minutes, then to 1 cup of orange peel add 1 cup sugar, cover with water and boil until syrup threads Take out of syrup and roll in sugar. Dry it.

Mrs F. M. Kilmer Jr.

BETTY'S CANDY
Good For Children

Two cups dark karo or molasses, 1 cup sugar, 1-4 cup flour or corn starch, 1-4 cup cocoa. Cook ingredients in iron skillet, stirring well to prevent burning. Cook until hard ball forms when dropped in cold water. Into pan, in which powdered sugar has been placed 1-4 inch deep, pour candy Furrows may be made in sugar so candy will form in sticks.

Mrs. W. L. Grigsby

MARASCHINO CHERRIES

Five pounds light colored cherries pitted. Four pounds sugar, stand over night. Boil until a syrup. Add red coloring and 1-2 of a 2 oz. bottle of almond extract and seal.

Mrs. F. M. Kilmer Jr.

CHOCOLATE FUDGE

Three cups sugar, 1 full cup milk, 2 squares grated chocolate, 2 tsp of cocoa, butter size of egg. Boil until it makes soft ball in cold water Partly cool before stirring. Add the butter just as it is removed from the fire.

Mrs. Jas. Westcott

DIVINITY

Use 2 pans, for first pan take 4 tbsp water, 1-2 cup sugar, boil until makes soft ball when tested. Second pan take 3 cups sugar, 1 cup of water, 1 cup white karo, boil until it makes a hard ball when tested in cold water. Beat 3 egg whites stiff, when first pan of syrup is ready add slowly to whites, beating steadily.

When all is beaten in, add second pan and beat til it begins to be as heavy cream, then add 1 cup chopped nuts and beat Pour in plate about 1 1-2 inch deep. Cut in squares.

Mrs. W. A. Barrett

TAFFY

Two cups sugar, 3-4 cups water, 1-4 cup vinegar, boil together until forms hard ball when tested in cold water, add 1 tbsp butter, 1 tsp of vanilla, pour in buttered plates and when cold take out and pull.

Mrs Annie Larned

FIG FUDGE

One fourth pound chopped figs, 1 pound brown sugar, 1 tbsp butter, 1 cup water, pinch of cream of tartar, 1 tsp lemon extract, pinch of salt. Chop figs, dissolve sugar and water, add butter and cream of tartar. When it boils add figs and boil till it forms a soft ball when tested, stirring all the time. Remove from fire and add lemon extract and salt, cool 5 minutes, then stir until to begins to grain, quickly pour in buttered pan and when cool cut in squares.

Margaret H. Hourihan

DATE CANDY

One pound of dates after seeding, 3 cups white sugar and 1 cup water, boil til it forms a hard ball when tested, take off stove and pour hot syrup over dates, flavor with vanilla and beat continually until thick, pour into buttered pan.

Mrs. W. A. Barrett

PEANUT BUTTER FUDGE

Two cups white sugar, 1-2 cup of milk and butter size of walnut, boil till forms soft ball when tested. Remove from fire, add 2 tsp peanut butter, beat until it begins to harden and pour into buttered pan.

Mrs. W. A. Barrett

AFTER DINNER MINTS

Three cups white sugar, 1 cup white syrup, 2 tsp water, 2 tsp vinegar. Set on back of stove, stir occasionally until sugar is melted then set over fire and boil until it forms a ball when tested in cold water, do not stir after begins to boil. Remove from fire and stir in peppermint to taste, pour in buttered pan and pull as soon as cool. Cut into pieces with scissors and roll in powdered sugar.

HONEY SQUARES

One cup strained honey, 1 cup of brown sugar, 2 tbsp butter, 1-2 cup cream, 1-2 tsp salt, pinch of cream of tartar, 1 tsp lemon extract.

Put honey, sugar, butter, cream and salt over slow fire and stir until dissolved, then add cream of tartar. Boil until forms a hard boil when tested. Remove from fire and stir in extract and pour in buttered tin. Mark in squares and wrap in waxed paper.

Margaret H. Hourihan

SEA FOAM CANDY

Three cups sugar, 1-2 cup red label Karo, 2-3 cup cold water, 2 egg whites, 1-2 tsp salt, 1 cup chopped nuts, 1 tsp vanilla. Boil sugar, water and Karo until forms soft ball in cold water. Pour slowly onto beaten whites of eggs. Beat till nearly stiff enough to hold shape, add nuts and flavoring and turn into buttered tin. Cut in squares when cold.

Leatha Riley

WALNUT FUDGE

Three cups sugar, 1 cup milk or cream, 4 or 5 tbsp cocoa, 1 tbsp butter, 1 tsp vanilla, 1 cup chopped walnuts. Boil sugar, milk and cocoa till it forms soft ball when tested. Take from fire and add butter, nuts and vanilla. Beat until thick and pour into buttered pans.

Leatha Riley

PENOCHE CANDY

Two cups brown sugar, 2 cups of white sugar, 1 cup cream, 3-4 cups Karo, cook until it forms soft ball in water, add 2 cups walnuts and 1 tsp vanilla, stir until creamy, pour into buttered pan and cool..

Edna Craig

———X———
COOKIES AND DOUGHNUTS

SCOTTISH FRANCIS

Three eggs, 1 1-2 cups sugar, 2 tbsp melted butter, 3 cups rolled oats, 1 tsp salt, 3-4 tsp vanilla. Beat egg, add sugar, stir in other ingredients, drop by tsp on inverted pan. Brown in slow oven. To make variety, use 2 cups rolled oats, and 1 cup cocoanut.

WHITE SUGAR COOKIES

Four eggs, 1 cup butter, 2 cups of sugar, 2 tsp lemon extract, 3 tsp of baking powder, flour to make soft dough. Do not roll too thin or lay too close together. When brown wipe with beaten egg whites and sprinkle with sugar. Do not pack in cookie jar until cold.

Mrs. T. F. Spalding

DAD'S SOUR CREAM COOKIES

One cup butter, 2 cups sugar, 5 eggs, 1-2 cup sour cream, 1 tsp soda, 1 tsp vanilla. Beat whites and yolks separately. Add soda to cup of flour. Cream butter and sugar, add yolks and cream again. Add flour and soda and cream, fold in whites of eggs and add vanilla. Add enough flour to allow the dough to roll 1-4 inch thick. Bake quickly in hot oven.

Mrs. L. W. Grigsby

SWEET MILK COOKIES

One half cup butter, 1 cup sugar, 1 tbsp sweet milk, 2 eggs, 2 tbsp of baking powder, 1-2 tsp vanilla, flour to roll.

BEST EVER DOUGHNUTS

Beat slightly 1 egg and 1 egg yolk add slowly 1-2 cup sugar, 2 tbsp heavy cream, 3-8 cup milk and 1-2 tsp lemon extract. Sift together 4 times 2 cups flour, 1-2 tsp salt, 3 tsp baking powder and 1-4 tsp nutmeg. Combine mixtures. Toss on board, shape, fry in deep hot fat and drain on paper. For richer doughnut add 2 tsp melted butter.

Mrs. Nellie C. McMurray

OATMEAL COOKIES

One cup fat, 1 cup sugar 2 cups of flour, 2 cups oatmeal, 2 eggs, 4 tbsp milk, 1-2 tsp soda, 1 cup chopped nuts, 1 cup raisins, 1 tsp cinnamon, 1-2 tsp clover, 1-2 tsp salt, mix and roll out in sheet and cut in squares with sharp knife.

Mrs. Nellie McMurray

FRIVOLETIES

Beat 1 egg white until stiff and dry and add 2 1-2 tbsp of powdered sugar, 1 tsp lemon juice, 1-3 cup of chopped walnuts, 2 tbsp raspberry jam. Pile by spoonsful in saltines and bake 10 minutes in moderate oven.

OLD FASHION SUGAR COOKIES

Cream 1 cup butter, 2 cups sugar, when well blended add 3 eggs and beat. Add 1-3 cup milk, mix and sift 2 1-2 cups flour, 2 tsp baking powder. 1-2 tsp salt, 1-4 tsp mace and cinnamon, add to liquid mixture. Add more flour if necessary. Roll on the board to 1-2 inch thickness and cut. Sprinkle with sugar and bake in hot oven 8 to 10 minutes.

Mrs. Frank Fitzgerald

DOROTHY'S CHOCOLATE COOKY

One cup light brown sugar, 1-2 cup butter, 1 egg, 1-2 cup milk, 1 1-2 cup sifted flour, 1 tsp baking powder. 2 squares melted chocolate, 1 tsp vanilla. Mix in order given and drop on floured pans and bake in hot oven 10 to 15 minutes. If frosting is desired use 1 cup powdered sugar, 2 tsp cocoa 2 tbsp butter, 2 tbsp black coffee, 1 tsp vanilla.

ICE BOX COOKIES

One cup brown sugar. 1 cup white sugar, 1 1-2 cup melted crisco or shortening, 4 1-2 cups flour sifted twice, 3 eggs well beaten, 2 tsp baking powder. 1 tsp soda. 1 tsp of cinnamon or other spices, 1 tsp of salt, 1 cup chopped nuts or raisins. Mix sugar and shortening, add eggs beat in little at a time beating. Add nuts last Make into long round loaf and place in pan lined with oil paper. Set in ice box or in cold place oven night. In morning slice as thin as possible and bake in quick oven.

Mrs. C. M. Jones

FRUIT SNAPS

One and one half cup sugar, 1 cup butter, 1-2 cup molasses, 1 cup raisins, 2 cups currants, 3 well beaten eggs, 1 tsp soda, 1 tbsp baking powder, 1 tbsp ginger, cinnamon and allspice, flour to make stiff dough. Drop by spoonsful on buttered tin. allow for spreading.

D. E. B.

SPONGE DROPS SOUTHERN

Four egg whites, 4 egg yolks, 1 tbsp lemon juice, 1 cup sugar. 1 cup cake flour, rind of lemon grated. Beat egg whites very stiff, add sugar

slowly, beat again until the sugar is dissolved, then add beaten egg yolks and sift the flour and cut into the mixture with a knife. Add lemon juice and rind. Bake in buttered muffin tins with circles of buttered paper in bottom.

Mrs. C. M. Jones

SWEDISH WAFERS

Cream 1-2 cup butter, 1-2 cup sugar, add 2 eggs. 1 cup flour measured before sifting. 1 tsp baking powder, 1 tsp vanilla. Drop from a spoon the size desired, sprinkle with shredded almonds. bake on upper grate in slow oven.

Mrs C. O. Gardner

DATE BARS

One cup sugar. 1 cup flour. 1-2 cup walnut meats, 3 eggs beaten, 1 tsp baking powder, 2 lbs dates stoned and cut in small pieces, a pinch of salt, 1-2 tsp lemon and 1-2 tsp of vanilla. Bake in sheet. cut into small strips. Sprinkle with powdered sugar.

Mrs C. O. Gardner

COCOA ROLL

Five tbsp sugar, 5 egg yolks. mix and cream 10 minutes, 5 tsp cocoa or chocolate. tbsp flour, 5 stiffly beaten egg whites. Bake in sheet 15 or 20 minutes in moderate oven. Roll in cloth when cool spread with whipped cream. Roll and frost with 1 square bakers cocoa or chocolate, melted. 1 cup powdered sugar stirred into 1 egg white, beat till all is smooth and flavor with vanilla.

Mrs. Wm. E. Quinn

FILLED COOKIES

One cup sugar, 1-2 cup butter, 1-2 cup milk, 1 egg, 2 tsp baking powder, 3 1-2 cups flour, vanilla and salt.

Filling:Two cups raisins, 1 3-4 cups sugar, juice and grated rind of 1 lemon, 1 1-2 cup boiling water, butter size of walnut, 3 crackers rolled thin. Cook until thick. Roll dough thin, cut and place small spoonful of filling on cookie. Place another cookie on top. Bake in quick oven.

Jeannette Lyons

BROWNIES

One cup sugar, 6 tbsp butter, 2

eggs, 2 sq. chocolate, 1-2 tsp salt, 1-2 cup flour, 1 cup chopped nuts, 1 tsp vanilla, 3 tbsp boiling water, 1 tsp baking powder. Cream sugar and butter, add eggs and choloate, dissolved in the hot water, then salt, flour, vanilla and nuts. Spread very thin in shallow buttered pan, bake in slow oven for 20 minutes, cut in strips, sufficient for 50 Brownies.

Mrs. Margaret H. Hourihan

HERMITS

One and one half cups brown sugar, 1-2 cup white sugar, 2 eggs, 1 cup sour cream, 2-3 cup butter, 1 tsp soda, 1 tsp baking powder, 1 tsp of cinnamon, cloves and nutmeg, 1 cup chopped nuts, 1 cup raisins. Mix as given adding enough flour to make stiff dough . Drop by tsp on buttered pans, allow room for spreading and rising. Cool before putting in ar.

Mrs. T. F. Spalding

CORN FLAKE COOKIES

Whites of 2 eggs, 1 cup sugar, 1-2 up walnuts, 2 cups corn flakes, 1-4 up shredded cocoanut, vanilla. Beat whites until dry, add sugar gradually and beat 2 minutes. Fold in corn flakes, cocoanut and nuts. Drop on greased pan, bake in slow oven.

Louise Stickney McNeil

SHREDDED WHEAT COOKIES

One cup white sugar, 1 cup brown sugar, 1-2 cup lard, 1-2 cup butter, 2 beaten eggs, 1 tsp soda in 1-2 cup sour milk, 3 cups flour. Roll 6 shredded wheat biscuits and add to mixture. Drop from spoon and bake in rather hot oven.

Louise Stickney McNeil

FUDGE SQUARES

Three tbsp shortening, 1 cup sugar, 3 tbsp chocolate, 1-8 tsp salt, 1-2 tsp vanilla, 1 cup milk, 1 cup flour, 1 tsp baking powder, 1-2 cup nut meats. Melt shortening, add sugar and unbeaten egg. Add chocolate, vanilla and milk, add flour which has been sifted with baking powder and salt. Add nut meats, mix well and spread thin on greased shallow cake pan, bake in slow oven 20 to 30 minutes, cut in squares before removing from pan. *agnes Potter*

1/3 cup milk

--------X--------

DANISH RECIPES

SPRUTBAKKELSER (Jiggers)

Yolks of 4 hard boiled eggs, 1 raw egg, 1 cup butter, 1 cup sugar, 3 cups flour. Rub yolks to smooth paste and mix with butter and sugar. Add raw egg and then the flour. Put through pastry tube, cut into four inch lengths and shape in the form of a capital S.

Mrs. Edvig Rasmussen

TVEBAKKER (Rusks)

Two cups flour 1 cup milk, 1 egg, tbsp butter, 2 tsp baking powder. Make as tiny biscuits and when cold cut and toast in oven.

Mrs. Alfred Fauerso

TWIBAKER

One half cup butter, 3-4 cup sugar, cup sour cream, 1-2 tsp cream of tartar, 1-2 tsp soda, pinch of salt, 1-2 cinnamon, flour enough to handle without sticking. Roll 1 tbsp dough in a ball and bake, cool, cut in half and bake again in moderate oven till crisp.

Mrs. George Petersen

DANISH COFFEE BREAD

One pint lukewarm milk, 1-2 lb butter, 5 eggs, 2 Fleischmann's yeast cakes soaked in a little water, 1-2 cup sugar, 1 tsp salt, 1 1-2 lb, or about 5 cups flour, butter for the pastry brush, cinnamon, sugar, Cardamon spice and chopped nuts.

Scald the milk. When lukewarm add the butter and the eggs, well beaten. Then put in the softened yeast, salt and sugar. Add enough flour so a soft dough is formed, as soft as can be handled with the hands. Grease with lard one side of a tea towel well. Place the dough in the center, bring the corners and sides of the towel to the top and tie, giving the dough all the room possible. Place the tea towel with the mixture inside a deep bowl one half full of cold water. The dough will sink to the bottom. Set aside over night or all morning to rise. When light, the risen dough will be found floating on top of the water. Then turn out quickly so as not to get any water into the flour, onto a well floured board. Cut into 5 strips. This amount makes 5 coffee cakes or part of the dough can be used for cinnamon rolls, for rusks or buns. Pat a roll flat with the hands and spread with butter, sugar and Cardamon spice. The spice and sugar should be mixed together to spread more evenly. The use of the Cardamon spice is not necessary but it improves the flavor immensely. Roll up the dough as for cinnaman roll and make a figure 8 of it in the pan. Butter the top and spread with nuts and sugar mixture. Snip the top at intervals with the scissors and arrange sections. Let the dough rise again. It will do so quickly this time. Bake in moderate oven.

Mrs Chris Nielsen

PARADISE PUDDING

Three eggs, 1 cup sugar 1 cup of dates, 1 cup nuts, 1 tbsp flour, 1 tbsp milk, 1 tsp baking powder. Bake 45 minutes in slow oven. Serve with whipped cream.

Mrs. G. K. Burgren

HOT MILK CAKE

One cup flour, 1 cup sugar, 1-2 cup milk, 2 tsp baking powder, 1 tsp butter, 2 eggs, flavoring. Beat whites of eggs stiff. Mix 1-4 of egg whites with yolks and sugar. and stir. Heat milk and butter and add to this mixture. Fold in egg whites and flour and baking powder.

Icing: Put one egg whites. 7-8 cup sugar and 3 tbsp cold water in the upper part of double boiler and set over boiling water. Beat constantly for 7 minutes. Remove from fire, add 1-2 tsp vanilla. and beat until thick enough to spread.

Mrs. Edvig Rasmussen

DATE TART

Stone and grind 1 package dates 1 cup chopped nuts. 1 cup sugar, 9 tbsp cracker crumbs. 1 tsp baking powder, 4 egg whites, added last. Bake in cake tin, cut in squares and serve with whipped cream.

Mrs. N. O. Nelson

ABELE SKIVEL

One half sifter flour, 1-2 tsp salt, 1-2 tsp soda, pour little hot water on to dissolve, yolks of 1 or 2 eggs,

sour milk or buttermilk to make a batter equal in consistency to waffle batter, sweet milk may be used, if it is, use 1 tsp baking powder instead of soda. Beat whites and add last. The griddle used has little separate round holes in which to cook each one. Grease with any kind of shortening, butter preferred. Turn them with a fork. A waffle iron may be used if the other is not available.

Mrs. N. O. Nelson

LAYER CAKE

One and one fourth cups sugar, 5 level tbsp butter, 3 egg yolks, 2-3 of cup milk 1 1-2 cup flour, 4 tsp baking powder, 1 tsp vanilla, egg whites.

Mrs. Alfred Fauerso

Lemon Filling: One egg, 1 tbsp butter, 1-2 cup sugar, 2 tbsp flour, juice of 2 lemons. Boil, stirring constantly.

Mrs. N. C. Jensen

SOSTERKAGE FRU SUR

One fourth lb sugar, 1-4 lb butter, 3 eggs, 1 handful small raisins, 1 pt. milk, 1 lb flour, 1 yeast cake, lemon flavoring. Mix the egg and sugar well. Melt the butter in the milk. Mix the yeast cake with a little sugar and luke warm milk. Add all ingredients to the egg and sugar and mix until it leaves the spoon. Put in well greased pan and allow to rise well. Bake in slow oven. It should take 3-4 hour to bake.

Mrs. A. W. Jensen

APPLE CAKE

Grease baking dish with butter and put a layer of bread crumbs, then several bits of butter here and there, add a layer of apple sauce and pieces of jelly. then bread crumbs and butter Bake in a very slow oven for about 1 hour .serve cold with whipped cream.

Mrs. Karen Ibsen

BOILED RAISIN CAKE

2-3 cup butter 1 1-2 cup sugar, 2 eggs. 3 cups raisins, 1 cup raisin water, boil and use when cool; 3 cups flour, 2 tsp soda, 2 tsp nutmeg, 2 tsp cinnamon. Bake in layers.

Mrs. Minnie Bogle

DATE CAKE

Two eggs, 3-4 cup sugar, 1 cup of

dates, 1 cup nuts, 1 cup flour, 1 tsp baking powder. This is very rich. It may be made into a loaf cake or rolled thin and cut into squares like cookies or bars.

VERY BEST SPICE CAKE

One and one half cups sugar, 1 cup butter, 2 eggs, 1 tsp soda dissolved in 1 cup sour or butter milk, 2 cups flour, 1 tsp cinnamon, 1-2 tsp each of cloves and nutmeg, 1 cup raisins, 1 cup chopped walnuts. Mix in the order given. Bake in square tin in moderate oven. This cake does not need frosting as it is moist and rich of itself.

Mrs Chris Nelsen

SMALL DANISH CAKES

One half lb. butter, cream, add a half lb. sugar and cream again. Add 4 egg yolks, 2 at a time, also small bits of fresh lemon peel. Stir well. Add 1-2 lb. flour, and last the 2 egg yolks and whites well beaten. Drop by teaspoons on pan and bake. Almonds or raisins may be used on top of each cookie if desired.

Mrs. L. P. Jorgensen

COOKIES

One and one fourth pound flour 3-4 pound butter, 1-2 pound sugar, 2 eggs, 1 tsp baking powder in a little water. Stir together as cold as possible. Roll out very thin. Sprinkle sugar and chopped almonds on top or brush with sugar and beaten egg. Bake in a moderate oven.

Mrs. Axel Nielsen

NATELKAGER

One scant cup butter 1-4 cup sugar, 1 egg, 15 almonds, 1-2 lb. potato flour. Mix and drop on pan. Bake until a light brown.

Mrs. George Petersen

PRUNE TART

One scant cup flour, 1 cup butter, very cold, cut together with knife, not touching with hands. Keep rolling out and out, not back and forth, till very thin. Cut in rounds, and bake light brown. Just before serving, place on each round a spoon of prunes that have been soaked, sweetened and mashed. On top of this put whipped cream.

Mrs. Pete Bebernes

————X————

FILLINGS AND ICINGS

ORANGE ICING

One egg white whipped stiff, add gradually confectionery sugar to make thick, fold in the grated rind pulp and juice of 1 orange.

CREAM ICING

Two cups sugar, 1-2 cup flour, mix and add 1-2 cup milk, butter the size of egg, boil until forms a soft ball when tested. Take off stove and beat until creamy. Flavor with 1 tsp vanilla. Use brown sugar instead of white, makes lovely caramel.

D. E. B.

CHOCOLATE FUDGE FROSTING

Two cups sugar 3-4 cups milk, 3 squares bitter chocolate, boil together until forms a soft ball when it is tested. Take off stove and drop in a piece of butter size of egg and 1 tsp vanilla but do not stir in the butter or vanilla until cold. Then beat until thick enough to spread.

PLAIN BOILED ICING

Boil together 3-4 cup sugar and 1-3 cup water, boil until it forms a soft ball when tested. Beat egg white very light, pour syrup in a fine stream over egg white and beat until it will hold its shape, flavor and spread at once.

MOCHA FROSTING

Cream 3-4 cup butter, add slowly about 3 cups powdered sugar, then enough strong black coffee to tint and flavor it.

LEMON FILLING

Cream together 1 cup sugar, and 1 tsp butter, add 1 egg and beat again, add juice of 1 lemon and beat all together. Boil 2 or 3 minutes, stirring all the time. Let cool before putting on cake.

O. E. B.

SEA FOAM ICING

Two cups brown sugar, 3-4 cup of water, Boil until is spins a thread, beat into whites of 2 eggs which are beaten stiff, add 1 tsp vanilla and 1 tsp vinegar. *mrs Jamieson*

MARSHMALLOW ICING

One and one half cups brown sugar, 1-4 cup butter, 1-4 cup hot water, boil until when tested it forms a soft ball in cold water. Add 1-2 pound marshmallows melted in a double boiler, then beat until thick enough to spread, add 1-2 tsp of vanilla.

PINEAPPLE FILLING

Beat 2 egg whites stiff, add slowly 1-2 cup sugar, then 1-2 cup crushed and drained pineapple, then add slowly and continue beating 1-2 cup sugar or enough to make filling thick enough to hold its shape.

Mrs. T F. Spalding

LADY BALTIMORE FILLING

Cook 1 1-2 cup sugar and 3-4 cup hot water until syrup spins thread. Pour syrup in a thin stream over egg whites beaten stiff and beat until light and fluffy. Save 1-2 icing for top of cake and to the other add 1-2 cup chopped raisins, 1-4 cup chopped dates. 1-4 cup chopped nuts. Use this as filling.

————X————

HOUSEHOLD HINTS

SCORCH STAINS

Lay a wet cloth over the scorched spot and iron over the wet cloth. If it does not come out try it again.

CLEANING KID GLOVES

Fresh sweet milk is better to clean kid gloves than gasoline. Dip cloth in milk and rub soiled places. Before gloves dry draw then out to prevent shrinking.

BLACK HOSE

Black stockings will always keep good color if after washing they are rinsed in blueing water.

BLACK SILK

For cleaning black silk use 1 tsp ammonia and 1 of turpentine to a pint of warm water. It will look like new.

BRASS

Tarnished brass when washed in the water in which potatoes have been boiled will be as bright as ever.

IODINE STAINS

To remove iodine stains from cloth, to a wash basin of water, add 1 tsp of coal oil, let article soak a few minutes, then stain will wash out immediately.

TO SET COLOR

To each gallon of hot water add 1 teacup salt. Put goods in water while hot and let set until water is cold.

INK STAINS

To take out ink stains in cloth soak soiled garment in sweet or sour milk several hours.

AXLE GREASE

To take out axle grease spots, apply lard or butter, then wash in hot soap suds.

CHOCOLATE STAINS

To take out chocolate stains, soak in cold borax water and pour boiling water through stain.

CAKE BAKING

To 5 pounds flour add 1 pound of corn starch. Use as any flour when baking cake. It makes them light and feathery.

TOUGH MEAT

To make meat tender add 1 tsp lemon juice or vinegar to water.

SPINACH

Put a little baking soda into the kettle where spinach is cooking and it will retain its green color.

TO COOK RICE

Add 1 tsp lemon juice to a quart of water in which rice is to be boiled will make the rice snowy white and keep the grains separate.

When making fudge drop 2 or 3 tsp molasses into the mixture, this keeps it from betting sugary and also gives it a better flavor.

GINGER COOKIES

They are better made with hot water than with sour milk, it makes them crisp.

FOOD CHOPPER
In running dates, figs, or raisins through a food chopper, add a few drops of lemon juice to prevent fruit from clogging chopper.

FOR BURNS
Use a mixture of raw linseed oil and soda.

STRAINER
To clean a fine strainer, take a bar of soap and rub the strainer thoroughly with this, then pour hot water through the strainer to carry away the soap and it is much better than using a brush.

FISH ODOR ON DISHES
A handful of salt should be added to a pan of water when washing utinsels that have contained fish and the odor will quickly disappear.

SPOTS ON BLACK SKIRTS
When cleaning spots from black skirts use a cloth dipped in water in which a little coffee and ammonia has been added. Iron on wrong side of material or over a damp cloth.

TO REMOVE MILDEW
Mildew on linen can be removed by wetting the marks, working soap into them and covering with chalk scraped into a powder. Work this well in and then wash the linen in the ordinary way.

A scented bag hung in a closet will keep moths away. Use the following spices: 1-2 oz. each of cloves, nutmeg and caraway seed.

A pinch of salt on a hot stove will drive away disagreeable odors.

To clean a polished table that has been marred by a hot dish, rub with camphorated oil.

When ivory has turned yellow, rub with turpentine to restore its color.

Sweet Disposition: Three grains common sense, 1 large heart, 1 good liver, plenty of fresh air and sunshine and 1 good husband. Don't boil.

To clean paint, put 2 oz. of soda in a quart of hot water, and wash with it, rinsing the paint off with clear water.

To cure Toothache: Heat 2 tbsp of vinegar. Dip a little absorbent cotton in the hot vinegar and apply to the gum at the root of the aching tooth.

---X---

ICE CREAM AND ICES

MAPLE PERFECT
Four eggs, 1-4 pt. hot maple syrup, 1 pt. thick cream, 1 tsp almond extract, salt and ice. Beat eggs separately and pour on them slowly the maple syrup. Cook until mixture thickens, cool it and add extract. When cold add cream beaten stiff. Mold and pack in salt and ice and let stand 4 hours.

PINEAPPLE SHERBERT
This quantity will make 2 quarts. Scald 1 quart milk, add 2 cups sugar, stir until dissolved and set to cool. When cold pack the freezer, turn in cold milk and let stand 5 minutes or until ice cold. Add strained juice of 3 lemons and 1 large cup of crushed pineapple with its juice. When sherbert is quite thick, add a meringue made with whites of 2 eggs and 2 tbsp of powdered sugar. If preferred, 2 tbsp of gelatine dissolved in 1-4 cup cold water, may be substituted for the egg whites. Work well together, repack and set away two hours to harden.
Mrs. C. V. Barker

FRUIT ICE CREAM
One half gallon thick cream whipped, 1 quart whole milk, 3 cups sugar, 1 tsp vanilla, whites of 5 eggs whipped stiff, 1 quart can of any fruit desired, added when cream begins to freeze. This is delicious. To serve 30 people.
Mrs. T. F. Spalding

GRAPE ICE CREAM
Sweeten 1 quart of grape juice to taste, add juice of 2 lemons, 2 cups sugar, put in freezer and when frozen mushy, add 3 pints cream whipped. 1 pint milk and 4 egg whites beaten stiff. This makes 1 gallon.
Mrs. W. A. Barrett.

PEACH CREAM SHERBERT

Four cups fresh extra ripe peaches mashed; add 1 cup sugar and let stand at least 3 hours to dissolve sugar, and bring out peach flavor. Freeze mushy and then add 2 cups heavy cream whipped stiff. Use strawberries, pineapple or raspberries in same manner.

Mrs W. A. Barrett

MOCK ICE CREAM

Boil 1-2 cup sugar and 1-2 cup of water until it spins a thread. To the syrup add slowly the beaten whites of 3 eggs. When cool add 1 pint of cream well whipped, add flavoring, pack in ice and salt and let stand 4 to 6 hours.

Glenna Smith Burhans

FIVE THREE'S

Three oranges, 3 lemons, 3 cups of grated pineapple, 3 cups heavy cream whipped, 3 cups sugar, 1 tbsp gelatine. This makes 1 gallon.

Mrs. T. F. Spalding

APRICOT ICE

One and one half cups white sugar, 1 quart water, 2 quarts apricots run through sieve, juice of 3 oranges and 3 lemons, 4 egg whites beaten up stiff. Boil sugar and water 5 minutes, cool, add apricots and juices. Freeze until mushy, add beaten egg whites and finish freezing.

Mrs. Margaret H. Hourihan

BANANA CREAM

One half gallon cream, whip well and add 3 egg whites beaten stiff, and 2 cups sugar. Place in freezer and when frozen mushy add 8 ripe bananas chopped fine. In like manner use any kind of fruit you desire such as strawberries, raspberries or pineapple.

D. E. B.

ORANGE ICE CREAM

Place 1 quart of milk in a double boiler and thicken with 3 tbsp flour and 3 cups sugar, when thoroughly done and cool, add the juice of 2 lemons and juice of 8 oranges and grated rind of 1 orange. Freeze slightly, then add 4 eggs whipped up thick but not stiff. Freeze. This will make one gallon.

+ 3pt cream whipped.

—————X—————

MISCELLANEOUS

CHEESE STICKS

One cup grated cheese, 2 tbsp of melted butter, 2 tbsp cold water, and flour to make stiff dough, using a silver fork to stir it with, until the mixture separates from the side of the bowl. Lay the mixture on a floured board and roll as thin as pie crust. Cut in strips 1-4 inch wide. Bake on a buttered cookie sheet or inverted pie tin in rather hot oven. Makes about 60 sticks.

RIBBON SANDWICHES

Take 3 square thin slices of white bread and 2 corresponding slices of whole wheat. Butter them and place between each two slices, the white bread being on the outside a filling made of egg paste. Take a sharp knife and cut crosswise into thin slices each five (three white and two whole wheat) slices of bread cut in to six sandwiches.

Egg paste is prepared by mashing yolks of 3 hard cooked eggs to a paste and adding 2 tbsp of salad dressing, salt and pepper to taste.

SALMON CROQUETTES

Remove bones and skin from salmon. To each can add 2 well beaten eggs and 1 cup mashed potatoes and 1 tbsp melted butter, and cracker crumbs enough to allow handling. Form in shape desired, dip in egg, roll in cracker crumbs and fry in deep fat. Garnish with parsley and slices of lemon.

Mrs. W. A. Barrett

SALMON ON TOAST

Flake 1 can salmon, remove the skin and bones, add to this 1 cup of milk in which 1 tbsp of flour has been mixed smooth. Add a little salt, pepper and butter. Boil 5 minutes, pour over toast and serve very hot.

Mrs. H. Stark

WHITE SAUCE OMELET

Three tbsp flour, 1-2 tsp salt, pepper, 2 1-2 tbsp butter, 1 cup milk, 4 eggs. Make a white sauce of the milk, butter, flour and seasonings. Separate the whites and yolks of the eggs and beat them until light. When the white sauce is cool, stir in the yolks and fold in the whites. Cook and serve like any other omelet.

BACON-EGG MUFFINS

Line the muffin cups with strips of bacon and break an egg in each cup. Place in the oven and bake until the egg is firm. Lean bacon is the best for this.

SANDWICH SUGGESTIONS

1.—Grind 1 cup nuts, 1 cup cooked ham, moisten with mayonaise.
2. 1 lb. cheese, 1 can pimentoes chopped, season and moisten with mayonaise.
3. 1 can tuna fish, 3 hard boiled eggs, 1-2 dozen sweet pickles, 1-2 cup nuts, chop fine and season with salt, celery seed, moisten with mayonaise.
4. Chop equal parts ripe olives and english walnuts, moisten with mayonaise.
5. Take hard boiled eggs, mince up fine and season with salt, pepper, moisten with mayonaise.
6. Take 3 hard boiled eggs. 1-2 lb.

cheese a few olives and a taste of onion minced fine. Season with salt and paprika and moisten with mayonaise.
7. Take cold boiled chicken, mince fine, add for each 3 cups meat, 3 pimentos chopped, 1 cup celery chopped fine, 1 pint mayonaise.
8. Grind 1 slice sweet onion, 3 hard boiled eggs, 1 pint chicken, 1 sweet red pepper, add season of salt and pepper. Moisten with 1 ounce of mayonaise.

Mrs. W A. Barrett

TABASCO EGGS

One cup heavy cream, 1 cup milk, 1 tsp salt, few grains cayenne pepper, dash of tabasco sauce, 6 eggs, 1-2 cup fine bread crumbs, 1-2 cup grated cheese, 6 toasted squares. Heat cream and milk in sauce pan, add salt, cayenne and tobasco, when it reaches scalding point, break in the eggs, dip the hot sauce over and around the eggs and when the eggs set sprinkle bread crumbs and cheese over and around them, if necessary add more milk, when eggs are done, serve each egg on a square of hot buttered toast.

Mrs Ernest Mankins

———X———

SOUPS AND CHOWDERS

CREAM OF TOMATO SOUP

Boil 1 quart tomatoes and 1 onion until well done and then run through sieve, season with salt and pepper. Heat 1 quart milk to boiling point, add 2 tsp butter, add to hot tomatoes 1-2 tsp soda, stir up well and add hot milk. Serve immediately with salted crackers.

NOODLES FOR SOUP

Take 1 or 2 eggs and add enough flour to them to make rather stiff dough, knead thoroughly, roll out real thin and cut in strips as fine as possible. Let dry a few minutes.

QUICK DUMPLINGS

Take the hot broth where chicken was boiled and pour over flour enough to make rather soft dough, roll out and cut in small squares. Cook quickly.

BARLEY SOUP

Take 1 small cup barley and boil

in 1 quart water slowly. Before cooking the barley, put soup meat on to cook 2 hours, as the barley thickens add soup stock salted to taste, if desired vegetables or lentils may be cooked with the soup meat.

VEGETABLE SOUP

Boil beef soup bone until well done, then set aside to cool and then skim. Add 4 potatoes, 1 large onion cut fine, 1-2 cup rice, 1 cup shredded cabbage and 1 cup of noodles. Just before serving add 1 small can tomatoes.

OYSTER SOUP

Pour 1 quart oyster liquor and all in a pan and simmer 15 minutes, thicken a tiny bit with flour, add 1 tbsp butter Heat 4 cups milk, season to taste, add to oyster liquor, serve at once.

SAUR KRAUT VEGETABLE SOUP

One lb. beef, 2 carrots, 2 onions,

1 green peppers, 1 cup saur kraut, 1 cup tomatoes, 2 turnips, 1-4 cup rice. Place meat in kettle, cover with cold water and cook slowly 2 hours. Add ingredients except tomatoes which are added 10 minutes before serving. No salt is added as saur kraut is salty.

Mrs. W. L. Grigsby

MONDAY SOUP

One cup baked beans, mashed in colander and heated with 1-2 cup of boiling water, 1 cup tomato puree thickened with 1 tbsp flour and 1 tbsp butter, 1 tsp salt. Add the thickened tomato to the hot beans and serve at once with croutons or crackers. Serves 4.

Mrs. Westcott

CLAM CHOWDER

Cut 3 slices of salt pork into pieces and fry till crisp. Add 1 quart of diced raw potatoes, 2 small onions. Cover with boiling water and cook until soft. Add 3 pints chopped clams and 4 soda crackers broken in small pieces. Season to taste, boil a few minutes and serve.

PARSNIP CHOWDER

Three slices fat salt pork or bacon minced and browned, 1 onion, minced potatoes diced, 1 pint diced raw parsnips, salt, 1 tsp, 1 cups top milk or thin cream and crackers. Put the minced vegetables into hot fat and cover with boiling water. Cook until tender. Add salt and milk and serve at once, hot. Six servings.

CORN CHOWDER BISQUE

Two slices bacon or salt pork diced an browned in good sized kettle, add in layers, salting each layer, 6 medium potatoes, diced, 4 medium tomatoes, peeled and sliced, or 1 pint canned tomatoes, 4 small onions finely minced, cover with 1 pint boiling water. Add 1 can corn. Cook 10 minutes. When ready to serve with crackers, add 1-4 tsp of soda and 1 quart hot milk which has been thickened with 1 tbsp butter mixed with 1 tbsp flour. Stir well. This makes 12 helpings When served with green salad, makes complete lunch.

——————X——————

SOUFFLE

TOMATO SOUFFLE

One cup tomato puree, 3 eggs, 3 tbsp butter, 3 tbsp flour. Cream the butter and flour and add the puree, stir over the fire until thick. Cook in double boiler 20 minutes. Add the well beaten egg yolks. Mix thoroughly and cool. Fold in the stiffly beaten whites of eggs and pour it into well greased pan. Set this pan into a pan of water and bake in very slow oven 1 1-2 hours, or in hot oven 20 minutes. The souffle is less apt to fall if cooked by the slow method. One cup grated cheese may be added before the thickened puree is removed from the fire. Let this melt and cool before adding egg yolks. Or 1 cup corn may be used with 1-2 of milk in place of the tomato and cheese, or add 1 cup milk to the mixed flour and butter and after it is cooked over the fire with constant stirring until thick, add 1 cup canned tuna fish, then use eggs as above.

Mrs. Westcott

VEAL SOUFFLE

One tbsp butter, 1 tbsp flour, 1 cup milk or meat stock, 1 cup of chopped veal, 1-4 cup bread crumbs, 2 eggs. Make cream sauce, add 1-2 tsp salt, and when cool add 2 egg yolks, fold in stiffly beaten whites. Bake 30 minutes in buttered pan, set in pan of hot water.

C. M. W.

CHEESE SOUFFLE

Melt 2 tbsp butter and 1 heaping tbsp flour. Stir in 1 cup milk, 1-2 tsp salt, speck cayenne, cook well, then add yolks of 3 eggs well beaten and 1 cup grated cheese. Let cool, add the beaten whites, turn in buttered dish, sprinkle paprika on top, bake 30 minutes. When done serve at once after removing from oven for will fall if let stand.

Mrs. C. M. Jones

TIME TABLE AND WEIGHTS

FOR BOILING

Meats (4 to 5 lbs) —2 to 5 hrs.
Fish (2 to 5 lbs)—30 to 45 min.
Ham (12 to 144 lbs)—4 to 5 hrs.
Corned Meat (6 to 8 lbs)—4 to 5 hrs.
Irish potatoes — 20 to 30 min.
Sweet potatoes —20 to 25 min.
Green Peas —20 to 30 min.
String Beans — 1-2 to 1 hr.
Young beets —45 min.
Onions —40 to 60 min.
Cauliflower —20 to 25 min.
Turnips or parsnips —30 to 45 min.
Carrots —1 hr.
Green corn —15 min.
Spinach —15 to 20 min.
Squash —20 to 30 min.
Asparagus —20 to 30 min.
Dice vegetables —20 to 25 min.

Mrs. Nellie McMurray

——o——

BAKING

Beef, rib (4 lbs- —1 hr.
Leg of lamb —1 1-2 hr.
Pork —3 to 4 hr.
Leg of veal —3 to 4 hr.
Chicken (3 to 4 lbs.) —1 to 1 1-2 hr.
Turkey (8 to 10 lbs) —2 to 3 hr.
Fish (3 to 4 lbs.) —45 to 60min.
Braise beef —4 to 5 hrs.
White bread —45 to 60 min.
Graham bread —30 to 45 min.
Cookies —8 to 10 min.
Cake thin — 15 to 30 min.
Cake, loaf —40 to 60 min.
Pudding, Indian —3 hrs. or more.
Bread pudding —20 to 45 min.
Pies —30 to 45 min.
Scalloped dishes —15 to 20 min.
Baked beans —12 hrs. or longer.

——o——

THICKENING AGENTS

1 level tbsp flour to 1 cup liquid for soups.

2 level tbsp flour to 1 cup liquid for gravies.
4 level tbsp cornstarch to 1 pint of liquid.
2 large eggs to 1 pint milk for custard.
1 egg to 1 cup for soft or baked custard.
1 level tbsp gelatine to 1 pint liquid.

LEAVENING AGENTS

2 level tsp baking powder to 1 cup flour.
1-2 tsp soda with 1 1-4 tsp cream of tartar to 1 cup flour.
1-2 tsp soda with 1 cup sour milk.
1-2 tsp soda with 1 cup molasses.

Mrs. Nellie McMurray

COMMON CUP WEIGHTS

2 cups lard	1 lb.
2 cups butter	1 lb.
4 cups pastry or barrel flour	1 lb.
3 3-4 cups entire wheat flour	1 lb.
4 cups graham flour	1 lb.
3 cups corn meal	1 lb.
4 3-4 cups rolled oats	1 lb.
4 1-4 cups coffee	1 lb.
2 cups granulated sugar	1 lb.
2 1-2 cups powdered sugar	1 lb.
3 1-2 cups confectionery sugar	1 lb.
2 1-2 cups brown sugar	1 lb.
3 cups meat (solid)	1 lb.
2 cups chopped meat	1 lb.
1 7-8 cups rice	1 lb.
2 cups raisins (packed)	1 lb.
2 1-4 cups currants	1 lb.

A saltspoon equals 1-4 tsp.
A tbsp liquid equals 4 tsp.
A tbsp dry equals 3 tsp.
A wine glass means about 1-4 tumbler.
A cup means a large coffee cup, not the small tea cup often used.
1-4 cup ground chocolate or 1 sq. chocolate equals 1 ounce.

——X——

PIES

ONE CRUST PIE CRUST

Three rounded tbsp of flour, 1 slightly heaped tbsp cold lard, a pinch of salt. Rub together until like fine crumbs. Add 1 1-2 tbsp cold water, mix and roll out, put in pan, prick sides and bottom with a fork and bake in quick oven.

PATTIE SHELLS

Three rounded cups flour, 1 heaping cup lard, pinch of salt. Rub together until like fine crumbs, add enough water to make soft dough. Roll out, cut with round coffee can lid and bake in gem tins. Prick side and bottom with a fork. This makes about 26 shells.

CHOCOLATE PIE

One cup sugar, 3 tbsp flour, 4 tbsp chocolate, 1 tbsp butter. Mix well and add 2 cups milk heated scalding hot, cook, then add 3 well beaten egg yolks, cook a few minutes, add 1 tsp vanilla, use baked crust and use 3 egg whites for meringue.

Mrs. Boyer

APPLE CUSTARD PIE

Three cups, milk 3 eggs, 1 cup sugar, 2 cups thick stewed apples. Strain apples through colander, beat eggs lightly. Mix with apples, add rest of ingredients, flavor with nutmeg. Bake with one crust same as any custard pie.

Mrs Nels Jensen

WALNUT FUDGE PIE

Put in sauce pan 1 cup sugar, 2 tbsp sweet chocolate, 2 heaping tbsp flour, 2 egg yolks, well beaten, 2 cups milk, and stir constantly until thickened. Remove from fire and add 1-2 cup chopped nuts, 1-2 tsp of vanilla and 1 tbsp butter. Have a pie crust already baked, pour into this the mixture. Beat whites of eggs stiff. Add 1/4 cup sugar, beat well, pour over the pie and brown in oven.

Mrs. Nels Jensen

PUMPKIN RAISIN PIE

One half cup raisins, 1-2 tsp salt, 1-2 cup milk, 2 tbsp sugar, 1 tsp cinnamon, 1-2 tsp nutmeg, 1 cup stewed pumpkin, 2 eggs, 2 tbsp molasses, 1-2 tsp ginger. Soak raisins in water until soft, drain and pass through food chopper, add to pumpkin, add to rest of ingredients. Mix thoroughly, then pour in pastry lined tin. Bake until center is firm, and serve cold. Makes one pie.

Mrs. Nels Jensen

SOUR CREAM PIE

Two cups sour cream, 1 cup seeded raisins, 1 tsp cinnamon, 1-2 tsp cloves, 2 cups sugar, 3 eggs. Beat eggs until light, add sugar and the spices and sour cream. Beat thoroughly and add raisins. Pour into a pie shell and bake same as custard pie. This will make 2 pies.

Mrs. Nels Jensen

HEAVENLY PIE

Line pie plate with pastry and bake. Mash 2 ripe bananas through potato ricer and add 1 cup sugar, 1-8 tsp salt and 2 unbeaten egg whites. Beat all together with egg beater until stiff and frothy. like egg whites. Add 1-8 tsp almond extract. Fill pie shell and bake for 20 minutes. Remove and chill and top with 1-2 pint whipped cream, sweetened.

Mrs. F. M. Kilmer Jr.

TEMPERANCE MINCE MEAT

Three pints finely chopped meat, 6 pints finely chopped apples, 1 pint chopped suet, 1 1-2 pints vinegar, 4 pints sugar, 1 pint New Orleans molasses, 2 pints water, 2 pints currants, 1 pint seeded raisins, 1 pint whole raisins, 3 heaping tbsp cinnamon, 2 heaping tbsp cloves, 2 heaping tbsp allspice, 4 pints sweet cider. Cook 4 hours and seal.

Mrs Step

PINEAPPLE PIE

Cream 2 well beaten egg yolks with 1 cup sugar, then add 1 tbsp flour stirred with a little water to a smooth paste. Add 1 cup of cream and 1 cup grated pineapple and bake in 1 crust. Lemon meringue on top and put back into oven to brown.

Mrs. Jessee Watson

SWEET POTATO CUSTARD

One pint boiled and pulped sweet potatoes, 1 pint sweet milk, 1 cup sugar, pinch of salt, 1 tsp lemon, 3 eggs, yolks beaten, sprinkle with nutmeg, bake in 1 crust. Use the 3 egg whites for meringue and set back in oven to brown.

Mrs. W. H. Ellis

PUMPKIN PIE

Two eggs, 1-2 cup white sugar, 1-2 cup brown sugar, 1 cup stewed pumpkin, 1 cup rich milk, 1-2 tsp vanilla, cinnamon and mace. Sprinkle top with cinnamon and bake in crust.

Mrs T. F. Spalding

GRAPE PIE

Fill bottom crust with ripe grapes, sweeten and dredge over it a little flour. When baked pour over it a sponge batter made of 3 eggs, 1 cup sugar, 1 cup flour, 3 tbsp milk, 2 tsp baking powder, pour over pie and return to oven and bake and brown slightly. Enough for 2 pies.

Mrs W. A Barrett

LEMON MERINGUE PIE

Two cups of water, 3 tbsp corn-starch, 2 tbsp flour, 1 cup sugar, 3 eggs, 4 tbsp lemon juice, 1 tsp of grated rind, 1 tsp salt.
Line pie plate loosely with pastry and bake. Mix flour, sugar and cornstarch with 1-2 cup cold water until smooth, mix in egg yolks, add slowly the boiling water, cook 5 minutes, stirring constantly, add the lemon juice, rind and salt. Pour in-to baked crust. Beat 3 egg whites, add 3 tbsp sugar and 1 tsp baking powder and spread thickly on top of pie, set back in oven to brown.

Mrs. M. T. McGee

CHESS PIE

Take 3 egg yolks beaten, with 1 cup sugar and 1 tbsp flour, add 1 1-2 cup sweet milk, 1 tbsp butter. Line pan with rich crust, pour in filling and bake. Use beaten whites for meringue and put back in oven to brown.

Mrs. T. F. Spalding

RHUBARB CREAM PIE

Cut enough rhubarb in small piec-es to fill a large cup. Take 2 egg yolks, 1 cup sugar, 1 heaping tbsp flour, butter size of walnut. Mix all together until smooth, then add the rhubarb and set aside at least 2 hours or until soft and creamy. Fla-vor with orange extract and pour in an unbaked crust and bake in a moderate oven until rhubarb is done, take from oven and pour over it the 2 egg whites beaten stiff with 2 tbsp sugar flavored with orange extract. Set back into oven to set and brown slightly.

Mrs. T. F. Spalding

CARROT PIE

Boil for 20 minutes, 3-4 cup grated raw carrots, 1-2 cup sugar, 1 cup of rich milk, and when cool add pinch of salt and ginger, 1-2 tsp each of cinnamon, cloves, 2 beaten eggs. Bake in 1 crust in moderate oven.

Mrs. N. O. Nelsen

COFFEE CREAM PIE

Three fourths cup strong coffee, 3-4 cup cream, 1-3 cup sugar, 1-3 cup flour, 3 eggs. Put coffee and cream in double boiler. Mix sugar and flour and drop into the hot liquid, beating rapidly with egg beater. When it thickens, add slowly beaten egg yolks and cook 5 minutes more. Pour in baked pie shell whites of 2 eggs for meringue

Mrs. N. O Nelson

BANANA CREAM PIE

Use same cream filling as above. Slice 3 bananas in a baked crust and pour the cream filling over the bananas. Use meringue on top, set back into oven to brown and as soon as taken out put several slices of bananas on top.

D. B. B.

MERINGUE PIE

Whites of 3 eggs beaten stiff, 1 cup sugar, 1 tsp vanilla, 1 tsp vine-gar. Mix all together and pour into buttered pie tin. Bake 40 minutes in slow oven. When cold fill with sliced bananas and top with whip-ped cream.

Mrs. Jos. B. Miller

GREEN TOMATO PIE

Into a pastry lined pie pan, slice green tomatoes very thin enough to fill plate, add melted butter the size of walnut, 1-4 tsp salt, 3-4 cup sugar and a little flour dusted over. Put on top crust and bake in medium oven.

Fernie Jamison

MOCK CHERRY PIE

One cup cranberries cut in half, wash in cold water and seeds will come out, then add 1 tbsp flour or cornstarch mixed with 1 cup sugar, 1-2 cup seeded raisins chopped, the juice of 1 orange, also a few nuts. Mix all together and pour over 1-2 cup boiling water. Cook through and boil and then add 1 tsp vanilla. Bake in 2 crusts or one with strips on top.

Mrs. C. M. Jones

VINEGAR PIE

To 2 egg yolks, add 1 cup sugar, mix and add 1 tbsp vinegar and 1 tbsp flour that is mixed to smooth paste in cold water. Add 1 tsp butter and boil until thick, then add 1 tsp lemon extract, put in baked crust and use beaten whites for meringue.

Mrs. H. F. Stark

VEGETABLES

PARSNIPS
Boil parsnips in salt water untill done, drain,pare and slice and place in baking dish with bits of butter over all, season with salt and pepper and set in oven until brown.

STUFFED TOMATOES
Cut off tops and scoop out pulp and seeds. Take pulp and mix with 1 cup chopped chicken, 1 cup cracker crumbs, 1 beaten egg, 2 tbsp of cream, 1 tsp onion juice, pepper and salt. Stuff tomatoes and pack in baking dish and pour chicken broth around them and cook untill the tomatoes are tender. Basting frequently with chicken broth is best. This will fill about 9 medium sized tomatoes.

Mrs W A. Barrett

CREAMED ONIONS
Cook small onions whole, then re heat in cream sauce made with 1 tbsp butter and 1 tbsp flour creamed together and added to 1 cup hot milk and cooked until creamy. Season with salt, pepper and bay leaf.

BAKED SQUASH
Cut into halves, take out inside, do not peel squash. Bake, take out of shell. Run through colander, add sugar and butter to season and put back in shell to serve.

BUTTERED CARROTS
Cook carrots until tender in salted water, drain off water and drop in pan containing hot butter and fry golden brown, turning over. Sprinkle with brown sugar and nutmeg.

EGG PLANT
Peel and slice egg plant and soak in salt water over night. Drain, dip in beaten egg, roll in cracker crumbs, fry in deep fat, garnish with parsley and slices of lemon and serve very hot.

BUTTERED BEETS
Cook young beets until tender, drain and skin, then chop fine or slice as desired. Put in pan, add salt, pepper and butter to season and just before serving add a dash of vinegar.

Mrs. Watson

STUFFED POTATOES
Bake long shaped irish potatoes. When done, cut off top and scoop out inside, mash and season with salt, pepper, butter and sweet cream, beat until light and fluffy. Put back in shell. Sprinkle with paprika and set back into oven to melt cheese placed on top. Serve very hot.

Mrs.T. F. Spalding

SPINACH
Pick, wash and place in large kettle with very litte boiling water salted. Boil until tender, about 25 minutes. Drain off water, season with salt, pepper and garnish with slices of hard boiled eggs.

POTATO CAKES
Six large raw potatoes, 2 onions, 6 eggs, 2 tsp baking powder, 1 level dessert spoon salt, 1-2 cup flour. Pare potatoes and onions. Wash and grate. Drain off water. Add flour, salt and baking powder, mix thoroughly, add eggs last. Fry in hot lard and butter to a golden brown. Very nice served with tomato catsup, stewd tomatoes or apple sauce.

Mrs. M. F. McGee

BAKED TOMATO HASH
Two cups cooked meat chopped, 1 cup bread crumbs, 1 1-2 cups canned tomatoes, 2 tbsp butter, 1 small onion chopped fine, salt and pepper to taste. Place mixture in buttered baking dish, with layer of buttered bread crumbs on top, bake till all is brown.

Mrs. Nels Jensen

FRENCH FRIED POTATOES
Take medium sized rather long potatoes and cut in long square shaped strips. Set in cold water a few minutes Drain off water and drop in deep hot fat and fry until a rich brown, stir often and do not cover kettle, when brown remove from skillet and sprinkle with salt.

CORN PUDDING
One can corn, 1 pint milk, 4 eggs beaten, 1-2 cup flour, large lump of butter, 1 tbsp sugar, salt to taste. Bake in earthen dish, serve hot.

Mrs, Jessee Watson

HOT SLAW

Shave cabbage very fine. Make a dressing of 2 egg yolks slightly beaten, 1 1-4 cup cold water, 1 tbsp butter, 1-4 cup vinegar, pinch of salt. Stir over hot water until it is creamy, add cabbage, do not let boil but lift cabbage carefully with fork until well covered with dressing and very hot. Serve at once, and it will still be crisp and delicious.

Mrs W. A. Barrett

STUFFED PEPPERS

Stem and scoop out centers and fill with a mixture of chopped chicken, cold roast, or other meat, chopped ripe tomato, bread crumbs. Bake until well done, take out and top with grated cheese, cracker crumbs and bits of butter. Set back in oven to melt, serve at once.

Mrs. T. F. Spalding

BOSTON BAKED BEANS

One quart beans, 1-2 lb. salt pork, 1 tbsp salt, 1-4 tsp pepper, 1-2 tsp of dry mustard, 2 tbsp molasses. Wash and soak beans over night. Put half into bean pot; wash salt pork and place in center; add remainder of beans, salt, pepper, mustard, molasses and 4 cups cold water. Cover. Put into slow oven and bake 8 hours. Add more water as needed.

Mrs. J. B. Miller

GLAZED SWEET POTATOES

Wash and pare 6 medium sweet potatoes. Boil in salted water 20 minutes. Drain and cut lengthwise, arrange in well buttered dish. Make syrup of 1 1-2 cups sugar, 2-3 cup boiling water, 4 tbsp butter. When syrup is thick, dip potatoes in syrup and bake until done. Baste often with left over syrup. Oven should not be too hot, as potatoes scorch easily.

Mrs. Step

ARTICHOKES

Cut off stem end, cover with boiling salted water and cook 1 hour. About 15 minutes before they are tender add a dash of vinegar. Serve with drawn butter or as a salad with mayonaise.

Mrs. Clarence Jones

SCALLOPED SWEET POTATOES

Two cups cold boiled sweet potatoes diced or sliced   1 1-2 cup of thinly sliced apples, 1-2 cup brown sugar, 2 tbsp butter, 1 tsp salt. Put in alternate layers in greased baking dish and bake 1 hour.

SUCCOTASH

Bean time and corn time'll soon be here,
If it ever gets round to the fall of the year,
Then git away with all of your trash
All I want is more succotash—

String and break green beans in 1 inch pieces, and boil in salted water with a piece of bacon, cook for 4 hours and about 3-4 of an hour before serving add 1 quart of green corn cut from cob and cook until tender.

D. E. B.

SPAGHETTI AND BEANS

One pint cooked string beans, salted, 3 cups cooked spaghetti, salted to taste, sauce made by simmering until thick, 2 or 3 slices of bacon cut up fine and browned, 6 tomatoes or 1 pint canned tomatoes, 1 tsp of salt, 1 tsp sugar, 1 small onion and 2 whole cloves. Mix spaghetti and sauce over fire until warmed. Serve with a green salad.

RICE CROQUETTES

Two tbsp butter, 1 tbsp flour, 1-2 cup milk, 2 eggs, 2 tsp chopped onion, 1 cup drained boiled rice, 1 tbsp chopped parsley, 1 tbsp chopped nuts and salt. Cream butter and flour, add the milk and stir over fire until it is thick and smooth. Add one of the eggs well beaten, the onion, rice and other egg hard boiled and chopped, and the rest of ingredients. Cool. Shape and roll in fine bread crumbs, beaten egg and in the crumbs a second time. Fry in hot fat.

SCALLOPED MINUTE TAPIOCA

Three quarters cup hot milk and 1-2 cup hot water in double boiler, 3 tbsp minute tapioca, 3-4 cup cooked fish or meat, 1 egg well beaten, 1-4 cup bread crumbs, buttered. Cook milk, water and tapioca 10 minutes. Add shredded or chopped fish or the meat and cook 10 minutes more. Add egg and salt to taste. Turn out in a well buttered baking dish, cover with crumbs and bake 1-2 hour.

BAKED CABBAGE

Cut up one small cabbage and boil 10 minutes. Drain and boil in fresh water until tender. Mash fine with fork and add 2 well beaten eggs, 1 tbsp melted butter, 1 tsp salt, 3 tbsp cream or milk. Place in buttered dish, sprinkle with buttered crumbs and bake about 30 minutes.

TENNESSEE CORN

One quart green corn, 2 eggs, 1 tsp salt, 1-2 tsp pepper, 2 tbsp of melted butter, 3tbsp cream, 1 cup of milk. With a sharp knife cut corn from cob. Heat milk, add eggs and seasonings, then butter and scalded milk. Place corn in buttered dish and pour the liquid mixture over it. Bake in slow oven. *till firm.*

Mrs. F. M. Kilmer, Jr.

SCALLOPED EGG PLANT

Peel egg plant and slice, then boil in salted water until tender. Pour off water and mash and mix with cracker crumbs, 1 egg and grated cheese with it; salt and pepper to taste. Put in baking dish grate cheese on top and bake until cheese is melted.

Mildred McMurray

VEGETABLE LUNCHEON DISH

One slice toasted bread for each person, 1 hard boiled egg for each, 1 cup cooked green peas. Cream sauce made of 2 tbsp butter, 2 tbsp flour and 1 cup milk. When this is boiling and thick, add 1 tsp lemon juice and salt. Make double this amount of cream sauce if more than 4 persons to be served. Dip the crusts of the toast into boiling water to soften and butter each slice. Place heaping tbsp of peas on each slice, cover with cream sauce, place on top of this the two halves of hard boiled egg cut lengthwise, cut side up and garnish with parsley.

Mrs. James Westcott

SPANISH AND ITALIAN RECIPES

ROUND STEAK ITALIAN

Four pounds bottom round steak, a *½ lb.* little suet, butter, and 1 can tomatoes, fresh tomatoes may be used. Render suet in pan, place butter and 1-2 onion in pan, when brown add rendered suet. Pound meat, rub with garlic, salt and pepper, nutmeg allspice and garlic. Place meat in kettle and when brown on both sides add 1 large can tomatoes. Let simmer slowly until meat is cooked, put brown paper between pot and cover to absorb steam. Strain tomatoes, add mushrooms to gravy for either spaghetti or Risotto.

Mrs. C. M. Jones

RAVIOLI

The paste is made by mixing 2 cups flour, 1-2 tsp salt, 2 whole eggs and 1-2 cup warm water to make a stiff dough, then knead until well together in a ball. Lay aside in a china bowl and prepare the filling. Two cups shopped cold chicken or of roundsteak. 1 cup cold cooked calves brains, 1 tbsp ground pork sausage, 1 sweet bread, 1-2 cup cooked spinach, chicken giblets and liver, 2 whole eggs, 1-2 cup parmassen cheese, 1 tsp Italian olive oil, dry mushrooms soaked. substitute veal for chicken. Grind add the ingredients through a fine knife, then add cheese, eggs, olive oil and enough bottom round steak gravy to make smooth paste, season with salt and pepper. Knead well 1-2 of paste and roll out like one would for noodles, set aside on clean board, then kneed out other half. Try and make them same size. Spread the filling not too thick, but even, when all covered, brush the whole with a white of an egg, then roll the first sheet on rolling pin and lay it over the meat covered sheet, and roll the ravioli rolling pin over the whole which will make little squares, then use pastry wheel to cut each square. Lift carefully off board and lay on clean cloth until thoroughly dry, turning them once. Have a large kettle of boiling water salted, place ravioli in carefully and boil until tender, drain well little at a time, place on hot platter, cover with Italian sauce and mushrooms, cover with grated parmassen cheese.

sprinkle *Mrs. C. M. Jones.*

POLENTA

Put in iron pot 6 cups water, 1 tsp salt and bring to boil. Stir into this 2 cups corn meal, 1 cup at time, stir with wooden spoon constantly to prevent burning, and cook until very dry and hard. Turn this out on bread board and shape and with a string cut hot mush into slices. Cov-

+ mold in rectangular shape

er bottom of baking dish with these slices, cover with grated cheese and dots of butter, season with pepper if desired, add another similar layer and brown in oven. Serve with beef stock or gravy.

N. Minetti

ITALIAN SPAGHETTI

One pound round steak, 1-4 pound pork ground through food chopper. 1-2 pint tomatoes, 2 large bell peppers chopped fine, 3 beans of garlic chopped fine, 3 medium onions chopped fine. Season with salt and chili pepper. Cook meat and all of above together. Have one pound of spaghetti in separate kettle, cooked. Add to the above when ready to serve. Add grated cheese last.

Mrs. C. O. Gardner

ITALIAN POT ROAST *noodles.*

In bottom of kettle put 1-4 lb. of butter, 2 tbsp lard, and bacon cut into small pieces. When hot add, finely chopped, 2 medium onions, 5 cloves of garlic, 6 sprigs parsley and mushrooms if desired. Brown pot roast, season with salt and pepper, add water and cook slowly until it is tender, add one slice lemon with peel removed, cook a few minutes. remove and discard. Add water from time to time as needed to make the gravy for noodles.

For noodles sift 4 cups flour onto board, in top of mound pour 7 eggs well beaten. With fingers work eggs into flour to make stiff dough and knead thoroughly. Roll into round shape, cover with bowl and keep this covered with a damp cloth to keep it this place damp cloth to keep mass moist and avoid crust forming. Let stand 20 minutes. Roll out into rectangular pieces so thin you can see through it. Rub over with flour so it will not stick. Roll up tight and hard and slice thin pieces off the end. Shake out until long and straight. Cook in boiling salted water about 20 minutes. Lift carefully from water into dish for serving. Cover with Monterey or Parmagiano cheese cut in small pieces and gravy from pot roast, add another similar layer, garnish with ripe olives.

Mrs. N. Minetti

RISOTTI, ITALIAN RICE

Clean Italian rice. Place in stew pot enough bottom round steak gravy to cover bottom of pot, add 2 cups rice stirring until rice is hot, add boiling soup stock slowly to more than cover. Boil slowly, stirring often, add more stock if necessary. Rice must be tender, all grains separate, when almost done, add more meat gravy and grated parmassen cheese and saffron. Steep saffron, a little pinch, in hot soup or hot water, use liquid only.

Mrs. C. M. Jones

TAMALE PIE

One pound round steak, 1-2 pound pork shoulder, 12 olives, 24 raisins, 1 tsp salt, 2 tbsp flour, 6 cups hot water, 2 tbsp fat, 1 cup cornmeal, 2 cups soup stock or hot water, 1-2 can chili sauce or 2 heaping tsp chili powder. Cut meat in cubes, fry 5 minutes ,add boiling water, simmer 1 1-2 hours, add chili sauce, salt, olives, raisins and last the flour mixed to a smooth paste in water. Melt fat in 2 cups boiling water, stir in corn meal slowly, cook 10 minutes, cool. Line deep dish or cassarole round sides, put in meat mixture, add little pats of meal mixture on top, place in oven 20 minutes.

Mrs P. B. Montanaro

SPANISH OMELET

Cover plain omelet with the following sauce: brown 2 tbsp minced onion in 2 tbsp butter and add 2 cups tomato, 1 green pepper cut fine, 1 tbsp flour, 1-2 tsp salt and simmer 10 minutes.

MACARONI WITH TOMATO PUREE

Two cups macaroni boiled in salted water, drain. Fry in 3 tbsp fat, 1 onion cut fine, 1 green pepper cut fine, add 1 small can tomatoe puree and take off and add 1 pound cheese cut in small pieces. Put in baking dish a layer of macaroni, then layer of tomato puree and cheese, repeat until dish is full, let last layer be of tomato puree then cheese, put in oven until cheese melts.

Mrs Virginia Ontiveros

PASTEL CHILENO

Take 2 dozen ears of corn and grate. Mix 1 cup of warm shortening, 1 cup sugar, 1 tsp salt, 1 cup of milk. Take 2 fryers which have been cut into small pieces and boiled. 1 quart olives, 1-2 package raisins boiled, put in pan a layer of the grated corn, then a layer of fryer, olives and raisins, then a layer of corn, etc. Bake in oven 1 hour. To be eaten hot.

Mrs. Virginia Ontiveros

SPANISH SANDWICHES

Mix 1-4 pound roquefort cheese with 1 tsp butter and 1-2 tbsp Worchestershire sauce. Spread this between thin slices of tart apples which have been cored and pared and cut 1-4 inch thick. Serve with crisp crackers.

Mrs. Virginia Ontiveros

ENCHILADAS

One half of 50 cent size bottle chili powder, 5 tbsp flour, mix together and add salt to taste, add enough cold water to make thin paste. Put in stew kettle, 4 tbsp shortening and heat, add above mixture, add 2 quarts warm water and stir well, let boil 10 minutes and set back. Take 1 quart flour, 1-2 tsp salt, 4 tsp baking powder, enough warm water to make firm dough. Roll out as thick as for pie crust, make from 12 to 14 and fry in deep fat. Brown on one side, then turn, brown and pile in dish. Take 2 pounds of cheese cut fine, 6 large onions cut fine, 1-2 package raisins boiled, 1 pint olives. Take each tortilla, dip in sauce, fill with cheese, olives, onions ,raisins, pour remaining sauce over, set in oven 15 to 20 minutes before serving to melt cheese.

Mrs. Virginia Ontiveros

SPANISH BEAN TURNOVERS

Take 2 cups cold boiled pink beans and put through food chopper. Turn this into hot fat in frying pan. Put 1 cup sugar and a little salt in. Let cool. Make a dough as follows, 2 cups flour, 1 tsp salt, 1 tsp baking powder. Mix with cold water to form stiff dough. Place small piece

of dough on bread board and roll thin in circular form, about 4 inches wide. On this put 1 tbsp of bean mixture, fold over 1 half and press edges together firmly. Fry until brown in deep fat.

To make Pelubies use this same dough recipe, roll them in circular shape, cut three or four small holes in each one and brown in hot fat. Serve with tea.

Mrs. Ramon Lopez

SPANISH NUT CANDY

Four cups brown sugar, 1 cup milk, 1 tbsp butter, 1 tbsp glucose, or maple syrup. Boil until it hairs, stirring as little as possible, then add flavoring and large cup of chopped nuts.

SPANISH CORN AND SQUASH

Nine ears corn cut from cob, 2 summer squash. Remove seeds and pare, 1 onion, 1 garlic, 2 green chili peppers, 2 cups strained tomato juice, 6 tbsp meat drippings, 1 tsp salt, a few grains cayenne pepper, put all together and simmer. Add a little water and cook slowly for 1 and 3-4 hours.

Mrs. Step

ABONDIGOS
(Little Meat Balls)

One half pound each of pork and hamburg, a little salt and pepper. Chop a small piece of onion and a green chili, also a tomato is desired. Add 1-2 cup bread crumbs, mix all together and make into small balls about the size of walnuts. Make a sauce in which the meat balls are cooked in for 15 minutes. Sauce: Put a small amount of lard in pan and into this put 2 tomatoes or 1-2 can, 1 green chili, 1 clove of garlic, 1 onion, a few mint leaves, all cut fine. To this add a little flour to thicken, about 1 tbsp and 1 cup water. *Mrs Bonnie Crabb.*

SALADS

ONE MINUTE MAYONAISE

One egg, 1-2 teaspoon mustard, 1 tablespoon vinegar or lemon juice. Break the egg in a bowl, put in salt, mustard and lemon juice. Beat all together a few seconds with Dover egg beater. Slowly pour in 2 cups of oil beating it in with other ingredients as it is poured in bowl.

THOUSAND-ISLAND DRESSIND

One cup good mayonaise, 1 teaspoon vinegar, 2 chopped hard boiled eggs, 2 tablespoons chopped pimento-stuffed olives, 2 tablespoons chili sauce, a little minced parsley, taste of minced onion if liked. Mix as used.

Mrs. W. A. Barrett

FRUIT SALAD DRESSING

Take 2 well beaten eggs, add 1-2 cup sugar and pinch of salt. Heat 1-4 cup pineapple juice, 1-4 cup orange juice and 1-4 cup lemon juice. Add to the egg mixture and cook in double boiler until creamy.

Mrs. T. F. Spalding

FRENCH SALAD DRESSING

6 tablespoons Wesson oil, 2 tablespoons vinegar or lemon juice, 1-3 teaspoon salt, a few shakes of pepper, a little paprika if desired. Stir well thoroughly mixing contents.

WHOLE TOMATO SALAD

Use 1 whole tomato for each person, cut slice from stem end of tomato and remove pulp. Chop fine some banana, orange, pineapple, or any fresh or canned fruit, and one small sweet green pepper. Mix and fill the tomato on top. Place 2 slices of cucumbers. Place on lettuce leaf and cover with rich cream, french or mayonaise dressing.

Mrs. C. R. Weston

CANDLE SALAD

In the center of a slice of pineapple (the candle holder) place upright a piece of banana 2 inches long (the candle). On the top of this place a tablespoon of sweetend mayonaise or whipped cream (the melted candle) and on top of this place a candied cherry (the candle flame). Serve on lettuce.

Mrs. H. S. Stark

CABBAGE SALAD

Shave fine 1 small firm head cabbage, season with salt and sugar. Add and mix lightly through 1-2 cup thick sour cream, also 2 tablespoons vinegar. Serve on lettuce leaves at once.

Mrs. W. H. Ellis

SALAD SUGGESTIONS

1. Place rings of canned pineapple on crisp lettuce leaves. Make balls of cottage cheese and ground walnuts. Place these in center of pineapple and top with mayonaise dressing.
2. Poinsettia Salad. Lay slices of canned pineapple on hearts of lettuce. Fill the centers with Kraft cheese mixed with mayonaise dress-

ing. Lay strips of pimento in wheel effect on the top.
3. Chop cabbage fine, add 1-3 as much minced pineapple, 1 dozen marshmallows cut fine and a cup of broken nut meats. Use 3-4 part of whipped cream to 1-4 part mayonaise dressing.
4. Raw Carrot Salad. Grate fresh carrots, 1 heaping tablespoon for each person to be served. Add Minced celery and nut meats. Or diced cooked potatoes may be added. Marinate with French dressing at least 15 minutes before ready to serve. Arrange on lettuce and serve with mayonaise.
5. Peel and halve lengthwise ripe bananas. Place the two halves face down on lettuce. Spread over with mayonaise and sprinkle over with chopped peanuts or any other nut.
6. Shred fine fresh sweet cabbage. To one quart of this add one cup finely chopped peanuts. Toss together with mayonaise and serve with water cress garnish.

HEAVENLY SALAD

This is delicious to serve at luncheon for a large number. Use 1 large can crushed pineapple. Stir into this 1 pound of marshmallows cut in small pieces. Let stand in a cool place for several hours. Then stir in one pound of chopped walnuts and 1 pint of whipped cream. Serve on lettuce leaves. This quantity should make 24 servings.

Mrs. C. V. Barker

SALADS

"To make a perfect salad, there should be a miser for oil, a spendthrift for vinegar, a wise man for salt and a mad-cap to stir it."

BETTY'S MACARONI SALAD

Into boiling water drop the macaroni. Boil rapidly and when soft, place in colander and pour over it cold water. Drain well and let cool. Cover well with salad dressing. Garnish with diced pickled beets and slices of hard boiled eggs.

SALAD DRESSING

Beat 1 raw egg, enough salad oil to thicken well. Add 1-2 teaspoon of salt. *enough vinegar to thin* This is fine for teething children.

Mrs. L. W. Grigsby

PUDDINGS, SAUCES AND DESSERTS

GRAHAM FRUIT PUDDING
1 1-2 cups graham flour, 1-2 cup molasses, 1-2 cup butter, 1-2 cup sweet milk, 1 egg, 1 teaspoon soda (level), 1 teaspoon salt, 1 cup raisins, 1 cup currants, 1 teaspoon cloves, 1 teaspoon cinnamon, and 1-4 teaspoon nutmeg.

Mix well together and steam 2 1-2 hours. (Serve with hard sauce.)

Mrs. William J. Phelps, Jr.

LEMON SPONGE
1-4 cup butter, 1 cup sugar, 4 tablespoon flour, grated rind and juice of 1 large lemon, yolks of 2 eggs well beaten, 1 cup milk, whites of 2 eggs well beaten. Cream butter, sugar and flour. Add lemon, yolks of eggs and milk, beat 1 minute. Then gently fold in egg whites. Bake in buttered pan set in hot water.

Maud C. Fox

CREAM PUFFS
1 cup boiling water, 1-2 cup shortening, 1 cup flour, 1-8 teaspoon salt, 3 eggs, and 2 teaspoons baking powder.

Heat water and shortening in sauce pan until it boils up well. Add all at once flour sifted with salt, and stir vigorously. Remove from fire as soon as mixed, cool and mix in unbeaten eggs one at a time. Add baking powder, mix and drop by spoonfuls 1 1-2 inches apart on greased tins. Shape into circular shape with wet spoon. Bake 25 minutes and cut near the base with a sharp knife to fill them.

CREAM FILLING
1 cup sugar, 1-3 cup cornstarch, 1-8 tsp salt, 1 egg, 2 cups scalded milk, 1 teaspoon vanilla. Mix the dry ingredients, add slightly beaten egg and stir into this gradually the scalded milk. Cook 15 minutes in double boiler, stirring constantly until thickened. Cool slightly and flavor. Whipped cream may be used instead.

Mrs. M. F. McGee

STRAWBERRY SNOW BALLS
1-2 cup butter 3-4 cup sugar, 1-4 cup milk, 2 cups flour, 4 egg whites, 2 teaspoons baking powder.

Cream butter, add sugar, milk and flour alternately; then the eggs beaten stiff, and lastly the baking powder. Put in small buttered cups and steam 1-2 hour.

Crush berries, cream 1 tablespoon butter and 1 cup sugar; add this to the berries. Pour over the balls and serve.

Mrs. Katherine M. Hill

CARAMEL PUDDING
1 cup sugar, melted in skillet, 1-2 cup sugar, 1-2 cup flour, 2 1-2 cups milk blended and warmed in double boiler, while sugar is melting. Pour mixture into skillet, stirring until thick and smooth. Serve with Whipped cream.

Mrs. N. O. Nelson

BROWN-SUGAR HARD-SAUCE
1-3 cup butter, cream butter, add 2 tbsp hot water, beat good and add 3-4 cup brown sugar, beating slowly until frothy. Flavor and set aside to mould. (Serve with hot pudding).

D. E. B.

BLACKBERRY ROLL
Make rich pie dough, roll out on board as thin as for pie. Cover blackberries. Sprinkle heavily with sugar, then a dash of flour and tiny bits of butter. Roll like a jelly roll and place in buttered pan. Pour blackberry juice about 1 inch deep in pan. Bake in moderate oven. When ready to serve cut in 1 inch pieces, lay flat on plate and pile high with whipped cream.

Mrs. W. A. Barrett

CHOCOLATE SOUFFLE
2 tablespoons shortening, 3 tbsp flour, 1 1-2 tsp baking powder, 3-4 cup milk, 1-3 cup sugar, 2 tbsp hot water, 1 egg, 1 1-2 squares of chocolate, 1-2 teaspoon vanilla.

Melt shortening, add flour and milk. Heat to boiling point. Melt chocolate, add sugar and water; stir until smooth. Combine mixtures, add well beaten yolk of egg and cool. Add baking powder and vanilla; fold in stiffly beaten egg whites. Turn into greased baking dish and bake in moderate oven about 1-2 hour. Serve with whipped cream.

Mrs. John W. Miller

MARSHMALLOW DELIGHT

1 pound best marshmallows
60 maraschino cherries
2 cups chopped nuts
1 pt. whipping cream
Enough sugar to sweeten
Beat cream until thick. Cut marshmallows into small pieces with scissors and add to cream. Add cherries and nuts and all the juice of cherries. Sweeten to taste.

Mrs. Edmond Fields

MAPLE PARFAIT

1 cup maple sugar
Yolk of 6 eggs
1 pt. of cream
Heat syrup to boiling point; pour onto beaten egg yolks and the whipped cream; turn into a mould and freeze. Serve with chopped brown almonds.

Mrs. Edmond Fields

AMBROSIA

Slice oranges and bananas, sprinkle with cocoanut, squeeze lemon juice over it. Serve with whipped cream.

Mrs. Edmond Fields

MERINGUES

Whites of 2 eggs
1-2 cup sugar
Beat the whites until very stiff and dry. Beat in sugar. Drop on butterd tins and bake in oven which is only slightly warm for 1 1-4 hours The baking is very important. They should rise and then brown. Cut tops and fill with whipped cream and sliced bananas or fruit in season.

Mrs. Edmond Fields

MEATS

Galey Twenty four

Meats

What to serve with meats:
Roast Pork: Applesauce or cranerry sauce.
Roast Beef: Grated Horse radish, Worcestershire sauce and pickles.
Roast Veal: Tomatoes or mushroom sauce.
Roast Turkey or Chicken: Cranberry sauce.
Roast Mutton: Currant Jelly.
Roast Lamb: Mint Sauce.
Roast Goose: Apple or cranberry sauce., currant jelly.
Corned Beef: Mustard.
Boiled Mutton: Caper sauce.
Boiled Chicken: Bread sauce.
Boiled Turkey: Oyster sauce.
Venison or Wild Duck: Black currant jelly.
Boiled fresh Mackeral: Stewed gooseberries.
Boiled Blue Fish: White cream sauce.
Boiled Shad: Boiled rice, Salad or lemon.
Fresh Salmon: Green peas, cream sauce.
Lobster: Salad Dressing.
Sardines: Sliced lemon.
Fish in General: Worcestershire sauce.
Ham: Mustard.
Fresh Cod Fish: Oyster sauce.

Boiled Beef: Horse radish.
Rabbits: Black currant jelly.
Pigeons: Mushroom sauce.

FLANK ROAST

Use 1 flank steak and have the butcher cut a pocket in it. Fill with good bread and onion dressing, salt and pepper and lard it well, sprinkling with a little flour. Brown the steak well in uncovered roaster and add 1 large 'cup hot water. Cover tightly and bake until tender, having enough water over it for gravy.

Mrs. F. Edelblute

CHOP SUEY

1 1-2 lbs. lean pork cut in 1-2 pieces
2 large onions
2 cups mushrooms
1 stalk celery
2 tbsps corn starch
4 tsps sugar
1-4 cup olive oil
3 slices bacon cut fine and fried
1 tbsp worcestershire sauce
1 cup warm water
1-2 teaspoon salt
Cut meat, mushrooms, celery and onions in small pieces.
Mix cornstarch with sugar in warm water, saute meat in bacon fat until well browned; then add vegetables and water. Cook 1-2 hour stirring

briskly, then add worcestershire sauce and serve with steamed rice.

Mrs. Toynette Wilson

BAKED HAM

Put a medium-sized ham in a pot and cover with sweet cider. Let it simmer gently for 3 1-2 hours. Skim frequently to remove the grease as it rises. When tender take out and remove the rind, cut the fat on top into diamonds and in each diamond stick a clove. Then rub over the top of the ham 1-2 or 1 cup of maple syrup. Bake slowly 45 minutes.

Mrs. M. F. McGee

ESCALLOPED FISH

3 cups any cooked flaked fish
1 cup fresh bread crumbs
2 cups cream sauce
2 tsp. finely chopped parsley or celery top, etc.
2 tsp. salt
2 tsp. butter
1 tsp. grated onion
Butter casserole, sprinkle in 1-2 bread crumbs, then fish crumbs and cream sauce. Bake without cover for 30 minutes in moderate oven.

Mrs. J. A. Westcott

CLAM TOAST

2 dozen small clams, 2 egg yolks, a pinch of salt, 1-2 cup scalded milk 8 slices of toast. Clean clams and cut into small pieces, simmer a few minutes. Beat the yolks of eggs, add slowly to scalded milk and combine with clams, adding salt and pepper to taste. Pour over the buttered toast on a hot platter, and serve at once.

Mrs. Nels Jensen

HAMBURG PIE

Mix minced hamburg cooked with tomato sauce. Pour in baking dish, top with baking powder biscuits. Set in oven until the biscuits are done. Remove and brush with melted butter.

Mrs. Wm. Step

VEAL LOAF

2 lbs. lean veal (chopped fine)
1-2 lb. salt pork (chopped fine)
2 cups buttered crackers (rolled)
2 eggs well beaten

salt, and pepper to tase
1-2 tsp. mace
Mold in loaf, roll in oil paper. Put butter over top and bake.

Mrs. C. O. Gardener

BREADED ROUND STEAK

1 pound of round steak ground and made into patties. Dip them in egg and roll in cracker meal, frying them in hot fat. Season with salt just before taking them out of frying pan.

Mrs. Harry Means

IRISH RAVIOLI

2 cups of chopped cooked meat, 1 onion, 2 eggs, 1-2 cup flour, 1 quart can tomatoes, salt, pepper, and red pepper to taste, 2 tbsp. butter, 1-2 cup drippings or lard.. Pass meat through chopper, add seasoning and one well beaten egg. Beat remaining egg, add pinch of salt and as much flour as the egg will take up. Toss on floured board and roll very thin and cut in 4 inch squares. Place an equal amount of meat on each square, add a bit of butter and press the 4 corners together. Place lard in sauce pan, add onion sliced and fry until brown. Add tomatoes and season to taste. When sauce is boiling drop in Ravioli quickly. Cov-10 minutes and serve very hot.

Margaret H. Hourihan

HUNGARIAN-GOULASH

1 large head cabbage, 1 pound hamburger, 1-2 cup raw rice, season with salt and pepper, a dash of ginger, mustard, paprika and cayenne pepper to suit taste. 1 large can of tomatoes. Take off leaf of cabbage carefully so as not to break them Place leaves in pan and pour boiling water over them a few minutes, then pour off-this is to wilt the leaves so you can handle them. Take meat, rice, seasoning and mix with hands and mould in balls a little larger than hen eggs. Wrap each ball in 2 cabbage leaves and pack carefully in pan so they will not unroll. Pour over all 1 large can tomatoes. Set in slow oven and cook 3 hours If broth cooks down, add water, and cover with another pan so it will not brown.

Mrs. W. A. Barrett

PICKLES, CONSERVES AND JELLIES

ORANGE MARMALADE
Wash 5 oranges and 1 lemon; slice very thin. To every pound of this add 3 pounds of water. Let stand 24 hours. Weigh and add an equal amount of sugar (about 10 pounds), juice of 2 lemons and one 20 cent can of pineapple. Boil until it will jelly (about 1 hour). Pour into jelly glasses and when cold seal with paraffin.
This will make about 15 glases.

Mrs. J. A. Westcott

CHILI SAUCE
12 large ripe tomatoes
3 large bell-peppers + 6 large onions
1 cup sugar
2 tbsp. salt
1 pint of vinegar
Peel onions and tomatoes and stem peppers. Chop all real fine, then cook with salt, sugar and vinegar until thick. Seal while hot in jars.

Mrs. Harry Means

PEARS PRESERVED WITH PINEAPPLE
Peel, core and halve pears and let stand over night with sugar on them. To 1 pint pears add 3-4 cups of sugar. Do not use any water as the sugar draws out the juice. Cook slowly until they turn pink and are thoroughly cooked. Then add 1 large can of pineapple. Heat to boiling again and can.

Mrs. W. A. Barrett

PEACH PICKLES
4 cups white sugar, 2 cups vinegar, 1 ounce stick cinnamon, 1-2 teacup pickling spices. Boil together for 20 minutes. Drop in whole cling peaches. Cook slowly until done. Pack in jars and cover with hot syrup. Seal.

Mrs. W. H. Ellis

CATSUP
To 1 gallon of tomatoes add 1-2 dozen onions and 1 dozen peppers. Cook well and strain. Discard some of the first water which you strain off, then add 2 cups brown sugar, 1 quart vinegar, 3 tablespoons dry Coleman's mustard, 2 tbsp. salt and 1-2 tbsp. of each nutmeg, cloves and celery sed. Cook until chick and bottle.

Mrs. C. M. Jones

RELISH
Boil beets until tender. To each quart of chopped beets, add 1 cup ground horseradish. Cover with vinegar and let stand a few days before using.

Mrs. O. A. Westcott

CRANBERRY JELLY
2 quarts cranberries, 1 pt. water. Cook and strain. For each pint of juice add 1 large cup sugar. Boil 5 minutes or until by testing it you see it will jelly.

Mrs. J. Watson

BERRY JAM
Pick over berries and mash up well. Heat to boiling point and add an equal quantity sugar. Cook slowly until the right consistency. Seal. Strawberries, raspberries, blackberries, loganberries, and gooseberries may be used in this way.

PEPPER HASH
Remove seeds and chop fine 12 sweet red peppers, 12 green peppers, 12 small onions, add 3 tbsp. salt and allow mixture to simmer 10 minutes. Drain and add 1 quart vinegar and 1 cup brown sugar. Let come to a boil and pour into jars and seal.

Glenna Smith Burhans

INDIAN RELISH
1 gallon small cucumbers sliced, 12 green tomatoes chopped, 12 onions chopped. Soak all in water over night. Drain and cook in plain water until tender. Add 1 1-2 qua...s vinegar, 3 cups sugar, 1 teaspoon black pepper, 1 tsp. celery seed, mustard seed and tumeric. Let come to a boil and seal.

Glenna Smith Burhans

JAM CHOP SUEY
3 lbs. rhubarb cut fine
3 lbs. sugar
1-2 pint water
1 lb. raisins
3 oranges cut fine
1-2 pound nut meats cut fine
Boil together 3-4 hours. Can. This makes about 2 quarts.

MUSTARD PICKLES

1 quart green tomatoes, 1 qt. cucumbers, 1 qt. small onions, 2 small cauliflower, 1 head celery, 4 red peppers. Chop and stand over night in a brine made of 1 pt. of salt and 4 qts. water. Then heat and drain. Dressing: 1 cup flour, 1 cup sugar, 6 tbsp. mustard, 1 tbsp. tumeric, 2 quarts vinegar. Mix flour, sugar mustard with a little vinegar until smooth, add rest of vinegar and cook until creamy. Put all together, heat thoroughly. Seal.

Mrs. M. Boyer

BOILED APPLES

Make syrup of 1 cup sugar and 1 1-2 cups of water. Let boil, add small bag of allspice(whole). Wash apples with skins, core or let stems be on. Jonathans are best. Put apples in boiled syrup and cover kettle. Let cook until skins are about to break. Then remove apples to dishes to be served. To syrup add a small wine glass of sherry, or grape jelly takes the place of this. Cook a little longer, then thicken syrup with 1 tsp. of corn starch, dissolved in a little cold water. Pour syrup over apples and eat while a little warm.

Mrs. C. M. Jones

CANTELOUPE PRESERVE

Peel outer rind and cut the meat of melon in inch pieces. Then for each pound of fruit add 1 tsp. ground ginger and 1 cup water. Boil from 10 to 20 minutes, drain off ginger water and add 3-4 lb. sugar to each lb. of fruit and return to fire and cook until tender. Thin slices of lemon will improve the flavor.

Mrs. Virginia Ontiveros

History is never complete. The included biographical material is, likewise, not complete.

There is no complete written history of the Santa Ynez Valley. Only fifteen of the 1250 issues of the Santa Ynez Argus are available in the holdings of the Santa Ynez Valley Historical Society. Cemetary records are notoriously inaccurate and newspaper obituaries have frequent typographical errors. Thus, much of our information comes from verbal accounts provided by some fifty living residents.

If you can help with additional information, clarification, corrections, or photographs for our second edition, please fill out the enclosed form at the back of the book.

Note:

Pythian Sister indicates membership in the Pythian Sister organization in Santa Ynez.

Census refers to the 1896 or 1898 Supplement Federal Census

SYVHS gives graduation year from Santa Ynez Valley High School.

BIOGRAPHY
OF
RECIPE CONTRIBUTORS

KATHLEEN "KATIE" ANDERSON (William)

Born: June 29, 1874 - Ireland
Died: December 31, 1966 (92) - Santa Barbara

Katie was married in 1902 to Bill Anderson, a Scots-
man. Bill and his brother, Jim, were the first
blacksmiths in Santa Ynez.

Katie was a widow when their first Santa Ynez
home burned down. Their garage (now Shannon's
Service) was used as parking for the high school.
(Parking was not allowed on school grounds.)

Their second home was located on Sagunto and is still
there. It was partitioned and used as a temporary
high school when the original school burned in 1908.

Katie and Bill had two sons, Jim and Jack. Jim was
a Santa Barbara Junior High School coach and still
lives in Santa Barbara. He married Marion Haugh.
Jack married Lenora Adams; he died in 1972. As of
1966, there were two grandchildren: Marleen Go-
forth (Harold) who lived in Red Bluff, and Wm.
Anderson, an attorney, who lived in Bakersfield.

Katie taught Myrtle Buell how to make bread. Her
fried chicken was so delicious her son, Jim consid-
ered marketing it. Unfortunately, her recipe is not
in the cook book.

1896 Census: Jim, the brother.

DEB

No information available.

MRS. C. V. BARKER

No information available.

DORA BARRETT (Wm. A.)

Dora moved to Santa Ynez from Los Angeles; she had
two sons, Ed and Bill, by a previous marriage.

She and her husband lived in the Jamison House which
later burned down. They also lived on the Armour
El Pioche Ranch (east of Wm. Kelly) where Bill was a
bookkeeper.

One son, Alfred "Chicken" Barrett, was married in
1939 to M. Emogene Wolf ("Mattie"); they had two
children, Jan and Tom.

Dora now lives at Oak Park in Santa Barbara.

Pythian Sister
SYVHS: Alfred, 1937

MRS. A. H. BARTH

She and her husband lived in Santa Ynez near the
Edward's family and may have built the Edward's home.
Later, they lived in the Ed Serge home.

Mr. Barth was principal at the high school in 1907
and 1908; they had one daughter and lived in the
valley only a short time.

MARGARET (NELSON) BEBERNES (Pete)

Pete Bebernes worked for McMurray Trucking.

Margaret and Pete had two sons, Vernon and Kenneth,
and one daughter, Gladys. Vernon married Bonnie
Lou Allbee, is a teacher in Santa Maria, and has

three children; Kenneth married Beverly Hudson and has three children; and Gladys married Stan Dukek and has four children. Kenneth is active in the Moose Lodge.

Pythian Sister
SYVHS: Vernon, 1938; Gladys, 1942; Kenneth, 1946

MINNIE BOGLE

The Bogles may have lived on the Mitchell Ranch.

MRS. J. C. S. BORGGAARD
(Listed as Mrs. G.K. Borgren)

Mr. Borggaard was a retired Danish minister, and they lived in Ballard on Alamo Pintado. They had two daughters.

MINNIE BOYER

Minnie Boyer lived on Refugio and later moved to Santa Barbara.

The Boyer's had a stationary thrasher which Frank Fitzgerald later purchased.

GLENNA (SMITH) BURHANS

Glenna was Frank Smith's daughter and the sister of Nellie McMurray and Irene Quinn. Her husband was a non-denominational minister who left the ministry and raised chickens.

She moved from The Valley to Humboldt County.

SYVHS: Glenna, 1908

CECILIA (MINETTI) COOPER (Robert L.)

Cecilia was the oldest daughter of Virginia and Umberto Minetti; she attended schools in Santa Ynez,
received her RN from Stanford Hospital, and later
worked in Santa Barbara.

She worked on the San Marcos Ranch, married Robert
L. Cooper in 1938, and moved to Merced.

While working for her dad in his Santa Ynez Market,
kids could buy a salami and cheese sandwich and a
quart of German lager beer. The boys competed with
one another, seeing who could drink a quart of beer
without removing the bottle from his lips. (Walter
Hartley could!)

SYVHS: Cecilia, 1926

THERESA COSTA

Born: October, 1873
Died: February 2, 1962 - Santa Barbara General Hosp.

Theresa was Mrs. C. M. Jones' sister. The family
came from New York; Theresa taught the mandolin and
played with an orchestra at The Potter Hotel in
Santa Barbara. She died in Santa Barbara when she
was 89.

ISABEL (MARIS) CRABB (Alonzo "Lonnie")

Born: 1856 - Santa Barbara
Died: 1943 (87)

Isabel married "Lonnie" on July 1, 1883. Her mother
was Dolores Chapman; her father, Capt. William Stevens Maris of Philadelphia. Her grandfather was
Joseph Chapman, who was born in Boston and died in
Santa Barbara in 1849. Joseph Chapman was in command
of one of Pirate Bouchard's ships and was captured in
Monterey in 1818. Her grandmother was Guadalupe

54

Ortega whose father owned the Rancho Refugio. Lonnie
Crabb's father was James Crabb and his mother, Hannah
Webb.

Lonnie and Isabel had a daughter, Blanche Anita,
born in 1890 in Santa Barbara and married to Alfred
John "Jack" Oechsel. They had a son, Jackie.

The Crabbs lived south of the Presbyterian Church
(now the Lutheran Church Shepherd of the Valley
Missouri Synod) on Lincoln Street in Santa Ynez.
Their home has been rebuilt to the previous style.

Lonnie was manager of several ranches, including
the Juan & Lolita, and was later constable and game
warden in Santa Ynez Valley. Lonnie's father was
later married to Giovanna Franzina who was from
Switzerland.

1896 Census: James Merritt Crabb

EDNA (RAYMOND) CRAIG (Elza)

Born: December 24, 1890 - Santa Ynez
Died: June 9, 1964 (73)

Edna's mother was Susan (Jamison) Miller Raymond
Bray. Edna married Elza on June 10, 1908 in Santa
Ynez. She was 17.

Their home stood toward the back of the lot where
the Red Barn Restaurant now stands. Mr. Craig was a
barber and also ran a bus service from Craig's
Pavillion To Santa Barbara. Craig's Pavillion
occupied the present site of the Red Barn and offered
midnight suppers and dancing. It was run by Edna
and Elza until his death in 1938.

They had two sons, Raymond (who died in November,
1963) and Fred ("Buddy") who lives in Santa Maria.

Edna played the piano, was said to be a very pretty
woman, and had a reputation for being a "good cake

baker." She was the second librarian in Santa Ynez
and served for 31 years - from 1929 to January, 1961.

Pythian Sister

EMMA ELLEN (FOSTER) DONAHUE (John)

Born: June 4, 1882 - Santa Barbara
Died: February 17, 1959 (76) - Lompoc

The Donahue's lived by the high school. Emma's
mother was Ellen (Burke) Foster and her father was
Marion Foster. Marion was superintendent of the Alisal and San Marcos ranchos.

Emma attended St. Vincent's Convent in Santa Barbara
and was married to John in 1902 at the Santa Ines
Mission. They lived on the San Marcos Rancho for
fifteen years; John was superintendent. They later
moved to their 65 acre ranch on Refugio.

John died in 1922 and Emma was chief operator for
the telephone company (after the Edsells) until 1932
when auto dial was introduced.

Emma and John had three children; Kathleen, Johnny,
and Mary Ellen. Kathleen married George C. Scoles
and had two children, Barbara Ann and John, and
lived in Fillmore. John married Edna Condit and
lives in Idaho; they had two daughters, Margaret
Mary and Nancy. Mary Ellen married Leonard Keck
and had two sons, Gordon and Thomas.

SYVHS: John, 1921; Mary Ellen, 1923; Kathleen, 1926
1896 Census: John Lawrence Donahue

FLORESA (REEDE) EDELBLUTE

When first married, the Edelblutes lived in Santa
Barbara on Montecito and Milpas. After they moved
to Santa Ynez, they lived on the corner across the
creek on Edison. Mr. Edelblute hauled freight with a

team in 1912 and 1913. They were later separated.

Floresa's mother was "Gramma Rud" (Reed); she smoked
a corn cob pipe and wore a poke bonnet. She had no
teeth. The children went by to say "hello gramma"
and after she had greeted them with a "good morning
children," they would stand around and watch her
smoke. She also sold homemade bread (little loaf-
5¢; large loaf - 10¢).

The Edelblute children were John, Eldo, and Eileen.

ANGIE MARIE (RICKER) EDSELL (Myrtle Buell's mother)

In 1909, Angie was the first telephone operator in
the valley. Their home was built on Pine Street in
Santa Ynez in 1897; it was later bulldozed. Mr.
Edsell also helped build the Santa Ynez Presbyterian
Church (now Lutheran Church Shepherd in the Valley
Missouri Synod) that same year. He owned Strahans
and Edsell Store in Santa Ynez; this building still
stands and the lettering can be seen on the east
side.

Mr. Edsell had a horse that loved to swim; it pulled
a buggy carrying Myrtle, her sister and sister's
child, and her mother across the Santa Ynez River.
(Myrtle couldn't swim.)

Their children were Myrtle, Hazel, Dorothy, Mildred
and Earl. Myrtle and Harold Buell were married in
1911 at Mission Santa Ines; they were the former
owners of the Indian Ditch Ranch in Santa Ynez.
Their children were Earl ("Buster") who lives in Los
Osos, Harold who lives in Phoenix, and Dorothy
"Dicksie" who married Fred Foxen. (In 1978, there
were 7 grandchildren and 1 great granchild.)
Hazel married Sam Kennedy and lives in Kern County;
Dorothy married Elza Foust.

Angie Edsell was not an exceptional cook but made good
chili sauce; Mr. Edsell was the better cook and taught
Myrtle how to make biscuits.

MRS. W. H. ELLIS

School Teacher

CECELIA (JENSEN) FAUERSO (Alfred)

Born: May 14, 1890 - Denmark, Kansas
Died: October 27, 1982 (92) - Solvang

Cecelia came to California in 1911 and she and her
husband were married in Solvang on October 30, 1912.
Their home, a two-story building on Mission Drive,
was the first built in Solvang.

Mr. Fauerso was a house painter; Cecelia was the
first music teacher in the Valley and had 75 piano
students. She travelled by horse and buggy as far
as Los Olivos in order to give lessons.

Cecelia's parents were H. P. and Maggie Jensen; she
graduated from Bethany College in Lindsburg, Kansas.
The Fauerso's instigated the Easter Sunrise Service
on Calzada Hill.

They had three children; Monica, Annette, and Phillip. Monica, married to Loel Kramer and still
living in Solvang, graduated from USC in 1935 and
was one of the first women to drive through Russia.
(1960.) Annette was first married to Frank Woodill,
then F. Ferrari and lives in Solvang. Phillip is
now deceased; he ran the Santa Barbara radio pro-
gram, "Nighttime in the Daytime."

In 1982, there were two granddaughters, Holly
Lindberg of Solvang and Lisa Chiesa who lives in
San Joaquin Valley, and one grandson, Steven Woodill
who lives in Chico.

SYVHS: Monica, 1930

EVA FIELDS (Edmund)

Eva was not from this area; she lived in Santa Ynez and, later, on the Los Alamos Ranch. She was a teacher.

Her husband, Ed, raised eight-horse teams and had a barn that could hold 200 horses. He used five teams for plowing the Zaca Ranch.

They had three sons; Ed, Jackie, and Jim. Jackie married a Santa Ynez teacher and had two sons. Jim Fields ran the first "bus" to the high school - a two-horse, four-seat spring wagon. (Jim Fields, Walter Hartley, "Nibbie"- the son of Llewellyn Fox, and Bill Downs hunted together.) Ed Fields had two daughters, Maud and Gertie.

Jackie ("Joey Gene") owns the Los Alamos Hog Ranch.

1896 Census: Edmund Fields
SYVHS: Jim, 1913

IDA (NEVIN) FITZGERALD (Frank)

Born: 1883 - Livermore, California
Died: December 18, 1950 (67) - Santa Barbara

Frank Fitzgerald worked on the Santa Barbara County Roads, and he and Ida lived in Santa Ynez in the Smith/Gardner house. The family is remembered for having (almost) a baseball team. The eight sons were: Kenny, Rolland, Dennis, Norman, John, Jim, Bill, and Eddy.

Kenny married Bessie May Ream in 1931; they own the Chimney Sweep in Solvang. Rolland married Alma Guidotti in 1935. Dennis married Katie Montanaro in 1937 and lives in Los Olivos. Norman married Althea Downs; they had two daughters and he is now deceased. John married Rena Hanson in 1947; they lived in Solvang and he is now deceased. Jim married a Main. Bill married Gladys Ross in 1946. Eddy married Betty Ann Reidel in 1947 and played professional baseball

for seventeen years. (Pittsburgh Pirates and Wash-
ington Senators.) All of these sons graduated from
College Grammar School in Santa Ynez and, later,
Santa Ynez Valley High School.

In 1950, there were seven grandsons and six grand-
daughters: David, Dennis, John Jr., Ken Jr.,
Michael, Pat, Pete, Catherine, Cathy, Claire, Linda
Ann, Melodi, and Rosalind.

SYVHS: Kenny, 1928; Rolland, 1928; Althea Downs,1935;
        Norman, 1936; John, 1940; Eddy, 1941; Bill,
        1944.

GLADYS (EDDY) FORBES (John)

Born: June 30, 1890
Died: July 14, 1978 (88)

Gladys was a nurse, and she lived on Refugio Road
next to the Abbot's home. She and John moved to
Santa Maria where he sold grain.

MAUD C. FOX (Llewelyn)

Born: August 28, 1876
Died: September 13, 1964 (88)

Llewelyn leased 3000 acres in Los Olivos from Judge
Canfield (where the Chamberlin Ranch is now). Maud
was a teacher at the Ballard School.

EVA (PRESTON) GARDNER (Chas. O.)

Born: February 18, 1863 - Castroville
Died: September, 1938 (75) - Lompoc

Eva's parents were Mr. and Mrs. E. J. Preston who
lived in Santa Ynez, Guadalupe, and Lompoc.

60

Eva and Charles had two children, Nellie and Jim.
Nellie married a McMurray; Jim now lives in Lompoc. (According to Myrtle Buell, when Jim was a
child: "he damned near killed me when he was
fooling around and hit me in the stomach.")

Mr. Gardner died in Santa Ynez in 1933, shortly
after he and Eva celebrated their 50th Wedding
Anniversary.

1896 Census: Chas. O. Gardner, Elijah Jackson
               Preston

SYVHS: Jim, 1912

LEATHA (RILEY) BRADLEY GREEN

Leatha's mother was India; her father, George Riley,
was general manager of mathieson's San Marcos Ranch.

Leatha married Jerry Bradley who ran the College
Hotel in Solvang; they had one son, Bobby. She later
married Mr. Green, and they lived in the house now
occupied by the Robert Parson family. She currently resides in Santa Barbara.

Fifty-four years ago, Leatha introduced Ken Fitzgerald to Katie on a blind date; she became Ken's
bride.

Walter Hartley made a Theodore (a "tie" in the old
days) for Leatha's father, and he "met a young
lady who talked him right out of it."

SYVHS: Leatha, 1927

KATE (ZIMMERMAN) GRIGSBY (Leslie W.)

Born: 1886 - Kansas
Died: November 9, 1947 (61)

Kate live in Solvang and Santa Ynez; Leslie taught

math in Los Alamos, then at the Santa Ynez High School.

Kate's father was John Calvin Zimmerman; her mother was Catherine Lee Zimmerman. John came to California in 1915 and to the valley in 1925.

Kate was a teacher in the Presbyterian Mission Schools in North Carolina, New Mexico, and Sitka, Alaska; she later organized her own school for the Chinese in Honolulu.

The Grigsbys had one daughter, Elizabeth "Betty", who graduated from UC in 1945 and married William Wiard, Jr. in 1947.

Pythian Sister
SYVHS: Betty, 1942

KATHLEEN M.(HOURIHAN) HILL (Ramon)

The Hills owned land in Santa Ynez on the mesa where the airport in now located. He ran the College Hotel by the Santa Ynez Park.

Kathleen's father was Mike Hourihan.

MARGARET AGNES (HILL) HOURIHAN (Mike)

Born: June 7, 1887
Died: June 4, 1955 (67)

Mike farmed east of Santa Ynez, on a grant from the Catholic Bishop. On occasion, he would be $20 on the Los Olivos/Santa Ynez baseball game.

They had four daughters and one son: Eleanor, Kathleen, Geraldine, Elise, and Lawrence. Eleanor married a Murphy; Kathleen married a Hill; Geraldine Pore lives in Santa Barbara; Elise "Babe" was a teacher at Santa Ynez Valley High School in 1944-46; and Lawrence lives in Santa Agueda Canyon in

Santa Ynez.

They lost their first baby to food poisoning;
it was thought to be caused by bad ice cream.
The Torrence baby died after attending the same
party.

SYVHS: Lawrence, 1933; Geraldine, 1936, Elise, 1938

MRS. KAREN IBSEN

Karen was a beauty operator; her husband was a con-
tractor. He built the H. Buell Ranch House which
was scheduled to be finished in January, 1922.
Shortly before the house was finished, he and four
other people were killed in an automobile accident.

The Ibsens lived in Solvang on the corner of Pine
and Laurel in a two-story white house. They had
two daughters; Esther married Bill Isaacson.

The Ibsen's 49 acre ranch was sold in August 1943
to E. T. Dunagan. Karen now lives in Lompoc.

SYVHS: Esther, 1930

FERNEY BELL (EDGAR) JAMISON (Sam)

See Page 79 for family chronology dating from 1831 to
early nineteen hundreds.

IONE (JAMISON)

Ione and her husband, Harold, farmed and lived in
Goleta. She was reported to be jolly and lots of
fun.

CHRISTINE (BURCHARDI) JENSEN (A.W.)

The Jensens farmed the Janin acres; she taught in
Solvang.

MILDRED (McMURRAY) JENSEN (Nelson)

Mildred was Nellie and Sam McMurray's daughter; she
was a singer, taught piano, and was a teacher at
the high school.

Her children are Margie, Helen, and Gene. Margie
lives in Solvang; Helen married Gerald E. Townsend
(Helen was also a teacher); and Gene lives in Solvang.

OLIVIA (GUIDOTTI) JENSEN (Nels P.)

Olivia was born in Lompoc in 1897; she later moved
to Los Alamos where she married Nels in 1919. In
1921, they moved to Santa Ynez Valley and worked on
the Mitchell Ranch for 21 years. Form 1948 until
1963, she lived on Calzada Street. Her husband died
in 1953.

Olivia's parents were Celestina and Louis Guidotti;
her brother, Mario ("Shorty"), married Florence
Fredericksen; her sister, Alma, married Rolland Fitzgerald.

Olivia lived in Santa Ynez from 1963 until 1977;
when she moved to Los Olivos to live with her niece,
Peggy Vernor.

Olivia once acted in the plays at Greer's Hall,
directed by Mrs. Weston.

Olivia and Myrtle Buell once prepared 68 lemon pies
and 68 pumpkin pies for the Rancheros Vistadores.
She feels her best recipe is her three-layer mocha
cake on Page 6.

Pythian Sister

MAGDALENA "MICKEY" ESTELLA (COSTA) JONES (Clarence M.)

Born: November 23, 1875 - New York City
Died: March 4, 1971 (95) - Taft

Mickey and Clareance ran a garage on the corner of Edison and Sagunto in Santa Ynez where she helped pump gas. Later, they lived on Refugio and ran the dairy by the river.

Before her marriage, Mickey travelled with a six-girl orchestra, on the vaudeville circuit. She came to Santa Ynez in 1916.

She and Clarence had two sons, Bud (Kenneth) and Ira ("Tip"), both living in Bakersfield; and one daughter, Mildred (Mrs. Harry Shumway) who lives in Cloverdale. In 1971, Mickey had seven grandchildren and two great-grandchildren.

Mickey Jones and Theresa Costa were sisters.

She made great Italian food, but none are included in the cookbook.

MRS. L. P. JORGENSEN

Her father-in-law was Carl Jorgensen, and they ran a grocery store across from Rasmussen's in Solvang.

They had two children, Ruby and Alex. Alex and his wife had a daughter, Alice, who married Milburn Pickner of Lompoc.

BEK

No information.

STELLA KILMER (Fred M. Jr.)

The Kilmers lived in Santa Ynez; he worked for the Santa Barbara County Roads. They were in the valley a short time before moving to Lompoc.

AGNES (POTTER) KLEINE (Henry G.)

Agnes lived on Refugio in Santa Ynez, and she taught
at the Solvang School. Her mother was a Lyons -
Jeannette was her aunt. Her father, E. F. Potter,
taught at Santa Ynez Valley High School from 1908
until 1914 and again from 1919 until 1923. He
wore a Van Dyke beard and high button shoes.

Agnes's sister, Frances Margaret, lives in San Diego
and, at 72, was recently married.

Agnes lives in Santa Barbara.

SYVHS: Frances Margaret, 1920; Agnes, 1925

ANNIE (JENSEN) LANG (Fred)

Born: August 8, 1890 - Jutland, Denmark
Died: September 18, 1973 (83)

Annie was Olivia Jensen's sister-in-law; she worked
with Olivia at the high school. Fred Lang worked
as an engineer on the Pacific Coast Railroad.

Annie's grandfather, Thomas Jensen, came to Nipomo
in 1890. In 1894, his wife, Dorothea, and two
children, Annie and Nels, came from Denmark and
joined him. Five children were born later; Charlie,
Christina, Mattie, James, and Mary. Charlie married
Leiala McCullum from Lompoc; Christina married
Julius Luis and then Bud Riley; Mattie married Laur-
ence Edie; Mary married Tony Serpa.

In 1898, they rented a portion of the Careaga
Ranch in Los Alamos and in 1904, they bought 482
acres from Sullivan and Roat, west of Los Alamos.

Annie's children were Alfred, who married Donna
Clark and had one daughter and then married Ann
Reggerio; and Peggy who married George Vernor and
lives in Los Olivos.

CLETA (LOGAN) LEWIS (William)

At nineteen, Cleta was married in Ballard by Judge
Lyons. She ran a millinery shop in Santa Ynez
with her sister and lived where the Red Barn is now
located.

Her daughters were Barbara, Verena, Martha, and
Laura. Barbara married Charles Troup; Verena
married a Cota; Martha married George Saulsbury;
Laura married Joe Alegria.

William Lewis came to the Santa Ynez Valley from
Visalia.

1896 Census: William Thomas Lewis
SYVHS: Martha, 1939; Joe Alegria, 1940; Barbara
       1942; Laura 1944

RAMOLI LOPEZ (John)

Ramoli and John lived on the Mitchell Ranch; then
on Manzanita Street in Santa Ynez. They had two
children, John and Lolita. Mr. Lopez died in
Lompoc and Ramoli remarried.

JEANNETTE LYONS

Born: November 7, 1886
Died: April 29, 1982 (95)

Jeannette's first teaching position was at Bloch-
man School in Sisquoc where she replaced a teacher
who could not handle the advances of several of
the twenty-six-year-old "boys." Jeannette was 18.
In 1909, she taught at Jonata School and was a
boarder at the R. T. Buell Ranch. Later, she worked
at the Ballard School and then at Solvang School
where she retired as principal. After retirement,
she ran the Feather Hollow Book Shop, east of
Ballard on Baseline.

Her father, Judge Sam, and mother, Myra, were very
active in Valley church activities. Many remember
Jeannette as their Sunday School teacher.

She was instrumental in establishing the Santa
Ynez Valley Historical Society with Grace and Edgar
Davison and Mary Gleason.

Two Lyons' homes burned down; the "old house"
(when her brother, Sam, was five), and in 1915,
two days before Sam's wedding, they lost a second
home to fire.

Jeannette was an imaginative and marvelous cook.

SYVHS: Jeannette, 1903

MYRA (WILSON) LYONS (Sam)

Born: January 15, 1847 - Pike Run, Washington County,
        Pennsylvania
Died: May 31, 1941 (95)

Myra married Sam Lyons on August 17, 1871. Her
mother was Rachael MacDonald, from Scotland; her
father was John Wilson from England. She was a
teacher when she was only 16 and made $25 a month.
She later earned $40 while "boarding around."

In addition to Jeannette Lyons, Myra and Sam had several other children: George, who was Forest
Supervisor for Modoc County (he died in 1929); Sam,
Jr. who was Captain of the California Fish and Game
and died in 1938; William, who ran a store in Cam-
bria; and Grace, who was married to Edgar Davison
and authored two valley-centered books - "Beans for
Breakfast," (1956) and "Gates of Memory," (1955).

68

RUTH (BLACK) LYONS (Sam Harrison)

Born: 1891 - Los Angeles

Ruth's parents were Robert and Clara Black.
Ruth studied law at USC and was in the same class
as Sam Harrison. (Sam used D.D. Davis' telephone
to call Ruth during their courtship days.)

Two days before Ruth and Sam were to be married, the
Lyons' home burned down; Sam was left with little
hair and no eyebrows for the ceremony.

Sam practiced law in Solvang until 1920. There
was no cemetery in the valley for Protestants;
the Lyons had lost their first baby (stillborn)
and Sam did not want cattle grazing over the grave
so he organized the first cemetery, now Oak Hill.

At the time of his retirement in 1938, Sam was
Assistant Chief of Patrol of the California Fish
and Game.

The Lyons had three children: Roberta, Jeanne,
and Sam Harrison, Jr. Roberta married Steven
Anderson; they live in Los Altos Hills. Jeanne
married a Marlin, was widowed, and now lives in
Mountain View; Sam Harrison Jr. is a retired Air
Force Colonel living in San Antonio, Texas. (Sam
Jr. was Dr. Hanze's first patient; the year was
1926 and Sam had scarlet fever.)

The Lyons left the Valley and lived in Woodland
California; Ruth now lives in Palo Alto.

SYVHS: Sam Harrison, 1907

EVA (LA BORBE) MANKINS (Ernest)

Ernest worked on the Doheny Ranch in Santa Ynez;
his father worked on the R. T. Buell Ranch.

Eva and Ernest had four children; Richard, Fred,

Maxine, and Loty.

Loty married Nielsen Downs. Richard married
Eleanor Grgich and they had four children;
Rick, Roseann, Francine, and Mary Ann. Richard
owns the Los Olivos Arco and Rick manages the
station.

SYVHS: Richard, 1943

MRS. M. F. McGEE

Mr. McGee drove for a trucking firm.

(This Mrs. McGee is not the Fannie McGee pre-
sently living in the valley.)

NELLIE C. (SMITH) McMURRAY (Sam K.)

Born: July 18, 1883 - Santa Ynez
Died: Febraury 15, 1941 (57) - Santa Barbara

Nellie was the daughter of Mr. and Mrs. Frank Smith
and was the first white child born in Santa Ynez.
She married Sam on September 3, 1902, when she was
nineteen.

She ran a rooming house in back of Craig's Pavillion where two or three local school teachers
lived.

Sam built Myrtle Buell's Lincoln Street House in
1919. The McMurray's moved from Santa Ynez to
Buellton where Sam later ran a trucking company.

They had a daughter, Mildred, and a son, Howard.
(Mildred married a Jensen.)

Under her leadership, the Ladies Aid Society began
the Valley Fair.

1896 Census: Frank Henry Smith
SYVHS: Nellie, 1901

LOUISE STICKNEY McNEIL

Teacher and later a nurse in Santa Barbara.

MAE (JAMISON) MEANS (Harry)

Mae's mother was Fern Jamison; they left the valley.

ELLEN (DECKER) MILLER (Joseph B.)

Ellen and Joseph lived in Santa Ynez across from the Anderson's (the house is still standing) and then moved onto the San Lucas Ranch. Joseph died of a heart attack and Ellen remarried Sam McMurray.

Ellen had two children: Robert and Alice. Robert ("Pete") married Rose Budd in 1942, and lives in Buellton. They have two daughters and a son. Alice married two times; Mr. Parker and then Charles Jones, and she now lives in Santa Barbara.

Ellen was reported to be a very good cook.

Pythian Sister
SYVHS: Rose Budd, 1940

MILDRED (DAVIDSON) MILLER (John Westcott)

The Millers had a ranch at the south end of Edison "under the hill." (The windmill and garage are still standing.) Mildred was a teacher at the high school in 1926-42.

Mildred's mother was Mrs. Elizabeth Davidson of Alhambra.

Mildred married John in January, 1926, in Riverside. He worked for H. H. "Tubby" Davis and on the Armour Ranch. He died when he was hit by an automobile at Refugio and Baseline.

They had one son, John, Jr.

VIRGINIA RAMONA (MARRE) MINETTI (Umberto)

Born: 1872 - Monterey
Died: August 22, 1951 (79) - Clovis

The Minetti's ran a restaurant hotel and hall in
Santa Ynez - Greer's Hall, where Mrs. Weston put
on many plays and community gatherings and dances
were held. (It is said Virginia would yell for
Umberto, and everyone knew when she had a customer.)

Their children were: Cecilia, Stella, and Henry.
Cecilia married a Cooper and lived in Merced;
Stella married Bill Barrett and worked in Sacra-
mento at the Courthouse; they have a son, Bill,
and a daughter, Kelly. Henry was a good basketball
player and later, a teacher in Bakersfield. He
married Margaret Hund, and they adopted a son, Richard.

Pythian Sister
SYVHS: Henry, 1921

MARINA MONTANARO (Peter B.)

Born: 1879 - Switzerland
Died: 1949 (70)

Marina was Swiss Italian; Grandma Crabb was her
aunt. Beginning in 1889, Peter sold meat through-
out the valley in a spring wagon and had stores
in Santa Ynez and Los Olivos.

They had three children: Katherine ("Katie"), Beatrice, and Arthur. Katherine married Dennis Fitzgerald and they had 2 sons, Peter and Michael.
Beatrice married Charles Raffetto. Arthur married
Alice Giorgi and ran the Los Olivos market following
his father's death in 1934.

SYVHS: Beatrice, 1925; Katherine, 1930; Dennis,

72

CHRISTINA (LETA) NELSON (N.O.)

Christina moved from Nebraska to Solvang to live with her daughter, Margaret Bebernes.

Mr. Nelson was very active in community affairs and politics. He enjoyed pinochle and croquet. Their home was always open, and she was a great cook.

ELEANOR (LABOREE) NIELSEN (Chris)

Eleanor taught music in Colorado and is the sister-in-law of Margaret Bebernes. Chris worked on the Duff Ranch.

They had three children: Ann, Esther, and Josephine. Ann lives in Santa Barbara; Esther in New York.

MARGARET (KNUDSEN) NIELSEN (Axel)

Born: December 4, 1904 - Wilbur, Washington
Died: March 16, 1978 (73) - Santa Ynez

Margaret and Axel ran a market in Solvang and lived on Pine Street. They had four children: Donald E., Roger, Lois, and David. Donald E. owns the Court of Four Flags Restaurant in Solvang; Roger is married to Ann and lives in Solvang; Lois was married to Kenny Cornelius and later, David Christensen and lives in Redlands. David Nielsen is deceased.

Margaret's brother, Karl Knudsen, lives in Solvang.

Pythian Sister

VIRGINIA (GONZALES) ONTIVEROS (Charles)

Born: January 10, 1884
Died: December 3, 1941 (57)

The Ontiveros family lived next door to C. O. Gardners on Sagunto in Santa Ynez. Charles' father was Patricio Ontiveros; Virginia's mother was a Ramirez.

They had seven children: Catherine, Alice, Rose, Refugio, Sophia, Ted, and Fred. Catherine married Andrew Mehlschau and lives in Nipomo; Alice married Ted Jensen and lives in Oakland; Rose married Carl Wasmund and lived in Santa Barbara; Ted lived in Santa Barbara; Refugio ("Mono") married Vela Williams and lives in San Jose; Fred lived in Santa Ynez.

Her daughters say her three best recipes are Sweet Bean Empanadas (served on Sunday afternoons), Palillies, and Enchiladas. The Enchilada recipe is on Page 41 in the cook book.

CLARA (NIELSEN) PETERSON (George)

Clara is Axel Nielsen's sister and lives in Solvang on Buellflat at Rancho Llano Grande.

She has two children; Robert and Bill, who own Buellflat Rock. Robert is married to the former Helen Holman; Bill to Myra Jensen.

BARBARA (MacGILLIVRAY) PHELPS (Wm. Jr.)

Born: December 13, 1893 - Los Alamos
Died: August, 1983 (89)

The Phelps lived in Los Alamos, then on a ranch in Los Olivos. Barbara was a high school teacher.

They had two children: William III and Ann.

Bill Phelps III married Betty and lives in Solvang.
They have two sons, Josh and Dave, and three daughters, Emily, Martha, and Nancy. Emily is married
to Larry Johnson, Martha is married to Michael
Nedegaard, and Nancy is married to Patrick Smith-
wick.

Ann married Ray McPeeters and lives in Santa Ynez.

Barbara's brother, Jack, married Dorothy Smart
and lives in Paso Robles and has a son, Fraser.

SYVHS: Jack, 1913; Ann 1940

IRENE (SMITH) QUINN (Willie E.)

The Quinns lived on Manzanita and Edison in Santa
Ynez. Shortly after their marriage, Willie was
killed in an accident with a horse, and Irene
moved to Santa Barbara. She was an active church
worker.

Irene had a daughter, Evalyn, and a son, Bitwell.
She was Nellie McMurray's sister.

SYVHS: Irene, 1902; Willie, 1904

GERTA (SKOV) RASMUSSEN (Edvig)

Gerta was a music teacher and later, baby sat. She
lived across from the grist mill in a two-story house
in Solvang. She had two sons, Thorvall and Albert.

SUSAN ALICE (JAMISON) MILLER RAYMOND

Born: October 31, 1862
Died: August 8, 1930

Susan married Elijah Ulysis Miller in 1880 and in
1882, they moved to Santa Ynez. They had two

children, Joseph B. Miller, who lived in Santa
Ynez, and Lorraine M. Smith who lived in San Diego.
Susan's husband died in 1885 and two years later,
she married Ulysses Grant Raymond. They had four
children, Edna, Richard, Irene, and Horace. Edna
married a Craig; Richard lived in Madera; Irene
married S. Hawkins and lived in Ventura, and
Horace lived in Ventura.

MRS. T. F. SPAULDING

Born:
Died: October 11, 1943

She was Elaine Mattei's mother; she moved from Woodland California to Los Olivos and lived in one of
the Mattei cottages on Nojoqui.

CHARLENE STARK (Hiram F.)

The starks first lived on Cota Street, next to the
Edwards; then moved to Refugio. Hiram worked for
the telephone company in Santa Maria; then in Santa
Ynez Valley.

MARY "MOLLY" (OLDS) BAILEY STEP (William)

Born: June 9, 1861 - St. Louis, Missouri
Died: October 5, 1953 (92)

She lived in Santa Ynez next to Fernie Jamison, then
on a ranch east of Cachuma. "Step" Creek ran into
Cachuma Creek and had excellent steelhead fishing.

Molly was born in St. Louis, Missouri and travelled
to San Jose in a covered wagon with her mother after
her father died. (1862)

She married George Bailey in 1879; he was a butcher.
They had two daughters, Mabel and Louise.

In 1893, the Baileys moved to Lompoc and in 1894, to a Santa Ynez Valley mountain ranch, and then into the town of Santa Ynez.

On December 27, 1900, Molly married William Step who had two children by a previous marriage; Elita who married Leo Hanley and lives in Santa Barbara, and Clarence who lives in San Fernando.

1896 Census: William Step
Pythian Sister

MAE (MAHONEY) TORRENCE (Frank)

Mae was born in Ireland; her two brothers were early San Francisco butchers. The Shepards live in the Torrence home in Santa Ynez, and have remodeled it. (Frank's sister, Alice Torrence, married John Cunnane. Their daughter, Margaret, married a Shephard.) Katie Anderson was Mae's cousin and Mae stayed with her in Santa Ynez when she came from Ireland.

Children: Hester, Audrey, and Mary. Hester, who lives in Los Angeles, didn't like horses but, coincidentally, her oldest daughter is a trick rider.

C.M.W.

No information

MRS. JESSEE WATSON

Her son, Ray, married former Mrs. Anna P. McNutt; he was an agricultural inspector for Santa Barbara County.

Her daughter, Madeline, married George Hartley and later, "Link" Wilson, and they live in Los Alamos.

The Watsons lived in Solvang.

SYVHS: Ray, 1928; Madeline 1929

DAVID WESTCOTT

David was James Westcott's oldest son; he graduated from Santa Barbara State (now UCSB) and currently resides in Walnut Creek.

David is the only male represented in this recipe book; this is because, at twelve, he was an excellent cook.

SYVHS: David, 1931

MRS. JAMES A. WESTCOTT

Mr. Westcott was principal of the high school from 1919 until 1931.

MRS. CLYDE (BROWNING) WESTON

The Brownings came from Pennsylvania to Los Olivos. Mrs. Weston put on many plays at Greer's Hall; Clyde was a barber in Buellton.

Children: Kenneth, John, Dorothy (Mrs. Ray Hubbard) who worked at the high school as a bookkeeper, Marie (Paul Maloney), and Charlotte.

Pythian Sister

ANISE (WATSON) WILLIAMS (Otha)

Anise's parents, Jessie and Melda, moved from Denver and ran a garage where the Red Barn is now located. Her brother, Bill, married Doris Sides who married a Young after Bill died. Anise has a son, Jack, who married Delma Ross and lives in Pasco, Washington. Anise' daughter, Mildred, married Winford Hull and lives in Walnut Creek. Anise currently resides in Santa Ynez.

SYVHS: Mildred, 1939; Jack, 1942; Delma, 1943

MRS. TOYNETT WILSON

No information available.

JOSEPHINE WINTER (Jessie S.)
(Listed as Jessie Winter)

Josephine was Mrs. Westcott's sister. She studied
in Europe and later became a Santa Ynez High School
Physical Education Teacher and Home Economics
Teacher (1929-33).

SYVHS: Josephine, 1923

JAMISON FAMILY CHRONOLOGY (dates approximate)

As one example of a family chronology from 1831 to the early 1900's, we present the Jamisons.

1831 - Tobias Jamison born in Allegheny, Maryland

1839 - Mary Elizabeth Cooksey born in Canton, Mo.

1848 - Tobias left Missouri; went down the Mississippi on a tramp steamer; around the Horn on a Clipper Ship; arriving in San Francisco in 1849.

1850 - Tobias travelled back to Panama; walked across the Isthmus; then back up the Mississippi River to Missouri.

1851 - Tobias crossed the U.S. in a covered wagon party with family members.

1857 - Tobias and Mary were married in Lewis, Missouri; they travelled together to California in a wagon party.

1859-62- In Redwood California, Santa Clara County, Tobias and Mary stayed with Samuel, Tobias' brother.

1865-67- They lived in San Jose

1868-71- Lived in Salinas

1874-80- Lived in Guadalupe and Betteravia; Tobias was Justice of the Peace and Supervisor of Santa Barbara County.

1880 - Came to Santa Ynez

1899 - Lived on Pine and Edison in Santa Ynez

1902 - Lived on Orella Ranch, Santa Barbara County

1906 - Mary Cooksey Jamison dies at age 67 at
     Naples (now Goleta)

1907 - Tobias dies at age 75 at Orella Ranch

CHILDREN: Sam, John, Warren, Susan, Ophelia, Mary,
     Josephine, Richard, Francis, Emma, Hannah,
     Tobias, Willie, Thomas

SAMUEL IGNACIUS JAMISON

Born: January 24, 1858 - Canton, Missouri
Died: November 2, 1924 - Santa Barbara County (65)
Married: October 31, 1888 - age 30 - in Santa Ynez
     to Ferney Bell Edgar. Sam and Ferney once
     lived in the Edelblute Home. (On a wagon
     trip, Sam became ill and his life was saved
     by Indians.)

JOHN HENRY JAMISON

Born: September 23, 1859 - Redwood, California
Died: October 11, 1920 (61) - Brinkerhoff Ranch,
     Santa Ynez
Married: November 4, 1902 - age 43 - in San Jose
     to Georgia Rawlings

WARREN COOKSEY JAMISON

Born: December 25, 1860 - Redwood, California
Died: June 9, 1910 - (49)- El Capitan, California
Married: December 18, 1889 - age 28 - in Santa Ynez
     to Alice B. Mills

SUSAN ALICE JAMISON

Born: October 31, 1862 - Redwood
Died: August 8, 1930 (67) - Santa Maria
Married: December 24, 1880 - age 18 - in Guadalupe
     California to Elijah Miller; later married
     Ulysses Grant Raymond; and in 1892, William
     Bray

OPHELIA

Burned to death at age 5 when her clothing caught
fire in a burning wheat field. (Probably in
Salinas.)

MARY SCOTT

Born: February 20, 1865 - San Jose
Died: May 26, 1954 (89) - Long Beach
Married: December 25, 1883 - age 18 - to Joseph
         Miller (brother of Elijah)

JOSEPHINE MARIA

Born: March 23, 1867 - San Jose
Died: July 8, 1934 (67) - Santa Maria
Married: May 1, 1888 - age 21 - in Santa Ynez to
         Ezra Grant Fields

RICHARD BELT

Born: June 26, 1868 - Salinas
Died: March 14, 1949 (80) - Santa Barbara
Married: November 25, 1895 - in Santa Ynez to
         Annie Ilenstine

FRANCIS MAY

Born: March 2, 1870 - Salinas
Died: January 15, 1948 (77) - Phoenix, Arizona
Married: November 3, 1891 - age 21 - in Santa Ynez
         to Alexander C. Ware

EMMA VANOY

Born: December 14, 1871 - Salinas
Died: November 9, 1958 (86) - Ventura
Married: June 4, 1902 - age 30 - in Naples
         (Goleta) to Horace W. Bickford

HANNAH (CHAPPIE) ELIZABETH

Born: March 19, 1874 - Guadalupe
Died: April 1, 1963 (89) - Ventura
Married: November 3, 1891 - age 17 - in Santa Ynez
         to William M. (Pop) Eddy

TOBIAS DILLON

Born: February 6, 1876 - Guadalupe
Died: January 1883 (6) - Santa Ynez (Diptheria)

WILLIE LOUISE

Born: November 27, 1878 - Guadalupe
Died: January, 1883 (5) - Santa Ynez (Diptheria)

THOMAS MacPHAUL ("MAC")

Born: May 17, 1880 - Guadalupe
Died: July 3, 1924 (44) - Madera
Married: June 27, 1906 - in Santa Barbara to
         Ellen J. Sullivan

Mary Elizabeth Cooksey Jamison was a Pythian Sister

1898 Census: John Henry Jamison

1896 Census: Ezra Grant Fields; Charles Ilenstine

1926 SANTA YNEZ VALLEY ADVERTISERS

LUDWIG ANDERSEN'S SHOE SHOP   Page 31

    Located in Solvang on south side of Main Street (now Copenhagen Street)

    Sold shoes and overalls

    Later run by Vic & Gladys Bruhn

    Now Viking Men's Shop

TONY AUSTED'S ELECTRIC   Page 37

    Located in Solvang on northeast corner of Main and 1st

    Now Solvang Shoe Store

THE CRAIG'S PAVILION   Page 7

    Located in Santa Ynez, present site of Red Barn Restaurant

    Dance Hall, Barber Shop, sold sandwiches

    Jake Stine had a restaurant here later

    During prohibition, it is "possible" Elza Craig had a pint for sale

DALLAS "D. D." DAVIS STORE   Page 13

    Located in Los Olivos on west side of Grand Avenue, north of the flag pole

    Groceries, hardware, work clothes, hats, candy, thread, yardage, etc. sold here

    Became "Bucket O' Blood Saloon" later

    Ora & Frank Cooper ran store after Dallas moved to Santa Maria. They tore buildings down and

Dallas "D.D." Davis Store Continued

Ora & Frank Cooper ran store after Dallas
moved to Santa Maria. They later tore
building down and used lumber for present
stucco house

H. C. HANSEN'S MEAT MARKET   Page 37

In Solvang on north side of Main Street,
next to Paaske's - Thumbelina Needle-
work is located there today

Carried Danish specialties

K. P. KNUDSEN'S CAFE   Page 4

Located in Buellton on Avenue of Flags
where used car agency was

Later moved to Solvang and became Sunny
Corner Restaurant, 1659 Copenhagen
Drive

JOHN MAXWELL'S EGGS   Page 33

Located in Santa Ynez, north of Cuesta
and Pine.

John worked at Santa Ynez Valley High
School as bus driver

MINETTI'S HOTEL   Page 35

Located in Santa Ynez on Sagunto, where
Joe Foss Real Estate in now. Several
small "guest"cottages are still standing. Greer's Hall (in back of alley)
is gone

Board and room, sandwiches, meat market
and store

NIELSEN & PETERSEN
Page 5

Located on northwest corner of Alisal
and Main, where Rasmussen's is today.
The store was larger than it is today,
with dry goods and groceries on east side
and women's department store on the west.
Margaret Bebernes and Ann Carlson worked
in the ladies side.

SANTA YNEZ FREIGHT LINE
Page 37

Located in Solvang. Proprietor was Sorn
Sorensen who was from Denmark via Austra-
lia. His speech was a unique combina-
tion of Danish-Aussie-American. He was
called Sorn "Two Times," "Chicken,"
and Sorn Post. He was a good cook and
later owned a baker and raised chickens.

SANTA YNEZ VALLEY NEWS
Page 31

Located in Solvang on the south side of
Main Street, where the Solvang Bakery is
today. Oscar L. Powell was editor in
1926.

SOLVANG FURNITURE STORE
Back Cover

Located in Solvang next door to Nielsen
& Petersen; it was owned by Terman Paaske.
It was later moved to east side of Alisal
where Lamplighter Shop is now located.

During funeral services, the furniture was
moved to the sides; there was also seating
in the front windows.

The funeral home was later moved to Buellton,
Santa Ynez (now Century 21 Real Estate),
then Ballard. It is now the Loper Funeral
Chapel.

86

Located in Solvang on the south side of Main
Street where Arnie's Restaurant is now.
The original building was burned down.

Carried boys and mens clothing and notions.

Mrs. Olsen and later, Andy Iversen, ran
the store.

INDEX

Note: Recipes end on Page 47; biographies begin
on Page 50.

Women are listed alphabetically under their
last husband's name. First names and maiden
names are included if known.

MANKINS,
  ELEANOR (BRGICH)   3, 28, 69
  ERNEST   68
  EVA (LA BORBE)   68
  FRANCINE   69
  FRED   68
  MARY ANN   69
  MAXINE   69
  RICHARD "DICK"   68
  RICK   69
  ROSE ANN   69

MARIS, DOLORES (CHAPMAN)   53
MARIS, CAPT. WM. STEVENS   53
MARLIN, JEANNE (LYONS)   68
MATHIESON   60
MATTEI, ELAINE   75
MAXWELL, JOHN V.   33, 84
McCULLUM, LEIALA   65
McGEE, FANNIE   69
McGEE, MRS. M. F.   12, 36, 43, 45, 69
McMURRAY, HOWARD   69
McMURRAY, NELLIE (GARDNER)   1, 6, 8, 20, 52, 60,
    63, 74
McMURRAY, SAM K.   63, 69
McMURRAY TRUCKING   51, 69
McNEIL, LOUISE STICKNEY   22, 70
McPEETERS, ANN (PHELPS)   73
McPEETERS, RAY   74
MEANS, HARRY   70
MEANS, MAE (JAMISON)   45, 46, 70
MEAT RECIPES   44
MEHLSCHAU, ANDREW   73
MEHLSCHAU, CATHERINE (ONTIVEROS)   73
MILLER,
  ELIJAH ULYSIS   62, 74
  ELLEN (DECKER)   5, 10, 18, 34, 38, 70
  JOHN, JR.   70
  JOHN W.   70
  JOS. B.   70, 75
  MARY SCOTT (JAMISON)   81
  MILDRED (DAVIDSON)   34, 38, 70
  ROBERT "PETE"   70
  ROSE (BUDD)   70

ACKNOWLEDGMENTS

So many people have helped; it is impossible to
credit all of them. To anyone I may have overlooked,
my apologies.

I have spent considerable time gathering oral
histories from the following:

Margaret (Nelson) Bebernes
Myrtle (Edsell) Buell
The Fitzgeralds
Walter Hartley
Beverly Jamison
Olivia (Guidotti) Jensen
Henry and Agnes Kleine
Kris and Olga Klibo
Jeannette Lyons
Ruth (Black) Lyons
Arnie & Amanda Meisgeier
Genevieve Murphy
Palmyra (Franzina) Murphy
Charlie and Eulalia Ochoa
Erlinda (Pertussi) Ontiveros
Barbara (MacGillivray) Phelps
Bill and Betty Phelps
Howard & Ruth Sahms
Hester Stonebarger
Peggy (Lang) Vernor
Anise (Watson) Williams
Cash & Dot Wolford

To the editor, Lynne Norris, heartfelt thanks
for her nimble fingers, spelling, patience,
and wit.

REPLY SHEET

NAME: _____

ADDRESS: _____

CITY:_____ STATE: _____

ZIP: _____ PHONE NO.: _____ _____

I have the following additions, explanations, corrections, etc., to add to The Cook Book:

I would like to order _____ copy(ies) of **The Cook Book** at $5.95 each.

My check for $ _____ is enclosed.

Please send order to: **Jim Norris**
                          P.O. Box 99
                          Los Olivos, CA 93441